C000271462

HAUNTED
TYNESIDE

The magnificent ruin that is Tynemouth Priory.

HAUNTED TYNESIDE

Darren W. Ritson

Foreword by Rupert Matthews

The History Press

*This book is dedicated to all the good people of Tyneside; past and present,
young and old, rich and poor, famous and infamous, whatever colour or creed.*

First published 2011

The History Press
The Mill, Brimscombe Port
Stroud, Gloucestershire, GL5 2QG
www.thehistorypress.co.uk

© Darren W. Ritson, 2011

The right of Darren W. Ritson to be identified as the Author
of this work has been asserted in accordance with the
Copyrights, Designs and Patents Act 1988.

All rights reserved. No part of this book may be reprinted
or reproduced or utilised in any form or by any electronic,
mechanical or other means, now known or hereafter invented,
including photocopying and recording, or in any information
storage or retrieval system, without the permission in writing
from the Publishers.
British Library Cataloguing in Publication Data.
A catalogue record for this book is available from the British Library.

ISBN 978 0 7524 5824 3
Typesetting and origination by The History Press
Printed in Great Britain

Contents

Acknowledgements

I would first like to thank renowned author on the paranormal Rupert Matthews, for kindly agreeing to write the foreword to this book. I would also like to thank my good friend Mike Hallowell for his friendship and support over the last ten years. Mike has allowed me access to his massive archive and library of ghost accounts that date back many, many years, and for this I am forever grateful. No one in the ghost-hunting world has supported me more than you Mike; you have my sincerest thanks. Thanks also to everyone I have spoken to in preparation of this volume; your ghost tales, accounts, and permissions for me to include them herein are most appreciated, and if it were not for folk like you, books like these may never be written.

My thanks go to those who have provided photographs and images for me to publish in this book: Bridon Ropes in Howdon, Walter Ritson, Colin Nunn, Mark Winter, Sheila Gascoigne and Mike Hallowell. Also to Sheila Gascoigne and Dr Nick Neave from the Sunniside Historical Society, for providing me with some great information about the Marquis of Granby. I must also thank my editors and staff at The History Press for their kind support and for their belief in me as an author. Special thanks go to Beth Amphlett, Matilda Richards and Anna O'Loughlin.

Finally, may I thank you, the reader, for choosing to buy this book. There are various books out there on the ghosts of the North East, so I extend my gratitude to you for buying mine. I feel you have made the right choice; I hope, after reading this book, you will feel the same way.

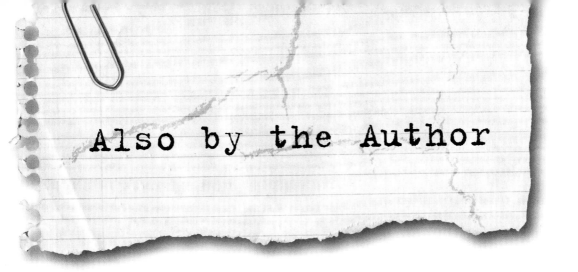

Also by the Author

The South Shields Poltergeist: One Family's Fight Against an Invisible Intruder
(with Michael J. Hallowell), The History Press, 2009

Haunted Newcastle, The History Press, 2009

Haunted Durham, The History Press, 2010

Haunted Berwick, The History Press, 2010

Ghosts at Christmas, The History Press, 2010

The Haunting of Willington Mill: The Truth Behind England's Most Enigmatic Ghost Story
(with Michael J. Hallowell), The History Press, 2011

Haunted Northumberland, The History Press, 2011

Foreword

IT was my wife who introduced me to Tyneside. Her father's family was out of Durham and she went to Newcastle University. She took me up to Tyneside for a holiday soon after we were married and I fell in love with the place. We have been back many times since.

As a historian, I made a point of touring the battlefields where the English and Scots clashed back in the Middle Ages: Halidon Hill, Homildon Hill, Flodden, Otterburn, Northallerton, Neville's Cross, Newburn Ford and many others felt the tread of my walking boots as I rambled around with a map in one hand and photocopies of old manuscripts in the other, trying to match the descriptions of the battle to the modern landscape.

But of an evening, I donned my ghost-hunting hat and set out to track down ghosts and other supernatural denizens of the area. Like Darren Ritson in this cracking book, I first went to the Grotto pub at Marsden. So when Darren invited me to write a foreword to his work, the first thing I did was turn to his entry on the Grotto to see what he made of the place. To my delight, Darren has got the place spot on! His description is just as I remember it, and his account of the hauntings is exactly what I was told. But Darren went much further than me; he stayed there overnight! I never had the courage for that.

He did just as good a job on the Red Lady of Cleadon Mill, another phantom I have gone to visit myself. So I eagerly plunged on into Darren's book; every page brought new excitement and wonders. I had heard of the South Shields Poltergeist before, but had no idea that it had been quite as dramatic and terrifying as Darren recounts here. Poltergeists are always disturbing, but Darren really manages to evoke the terror of this truly frightening event.

In this book, Darren takes us on a magnificent tour of haunted Tyneside. He leads us to some of the most eerie places in the area, treating us to some terrifying tales and disturbing stories, all told with an engaging charm. The ghosts, spectres and poltergeists pass by in endless succession, but, although what we read sends a shiver down the spine, the author manages to

The bridges of the Tyne at sunset.

pass on his information without disturbing us too much.

Some of the best-known haunted pubs around are explored, with startling results. The Black Horse at West Boldon has a particularly active spectre, while the Robin Hood at Jarrow has what seems to be a haunted clock. The Wooden Doll at North Shields has a rather disturbing watcher on the stairs – a ghost of which the author has had personal experience. He recounts the spooky event in these pages. Grand hotels such as the Angel View at Gateshead are not immune to paranormal activity either, for that hotel has some startling phenom-

ena going on. Much happier are the playful phantom children of the Tynemouth Lodge Hotel at Tynemouth.

And where would any ghost book be without a ruined priory haunted by an ancient monk? Tynemouth Priory fulfils that requirement here, and Darren passes on the first-hand account of a sighting from a friend, as well as recounting his own experiences. He takes us to less traditional haunted spots as well: a railway station, a nature reserve, and even the Angel of the North. It seems that wherever you turn on Tyneside, there is a ghost waiting for you.

I have been on the ghost-hunting trail myself for over ten years now. I have tracked down spooks in Scotland, spectres in Sunderland, phantoms in Kent and even fairies in Cornwall. Nowhere have I come across a better evocation of the supernatural world than in this book. Darren Ritson is an old hand at investigating the paranormal, and it shows in this volume. The skill with which he gets witnesses to talk of their experiences is impressive, while his own encounters with the unexplained are described with a clarity and good humour that is all too rare in writings about the paranormal – where too often truth is sacrificed to sensation.

If you are looking for a spooky read that is firmly rooted in reality, then this is the book for you. Even better, clutch this volume in your hand while travelling around Tyneside and stop off to visit the haunted pubs, theatres, cinemas and streets chronicled here. And while you are there, keep your eyes open; you never know when a ghost is going to jump out and scare the daylights out of you!

Rupert Matthews, 2011

Introduction

TYNESIDE; what a place to live and work. I was born in Newcastle General Hospital on 17 March 1972 and was subsequently raised in the St Anthony's (Walker) area of Tyneside with my brother Gary, my mother, Jean, and my father, Walter. My childhood home had spectacular views overlooking the River Tyne. Facing east along the river is Pelaw Fields and the neighbouring Bill Quay; facing west I could see the old Hawthorn Leslie factory, where my father worked for many years. Looking further west beyond Hawthorn Leslie's, which is now the stylish St Peter's Basin, one could see the magnificent city centre that is Newcastle upon Tyne, with St James' Park sitting nicely on the horizon, dominating the Geordie skyline. On match days, I often heard the roar of the 'Toon Army' as the magpies put one into the back of the net, and that was from two and half miles away, so you can imagine what the atmosphere was like inside St James' Park. To me, at that time, it was the best place on earth to live: I could see the Tyne, the 'Toon', and St James' Park, all from my back garden.

Tyneside is a place renowned for many a wonderful thing, including its engineering and steel works, which ultimately led to North East shipbuilding at the famous Swan Hunter Docks at Wallsend. Over 150 years of shipbuilding took place at the famous yard, with over 1,500 ships of various sorts being built, along with hundreds of other naval vessels; an amazing feat to say the least. In 1902, RMS *Carpathia* was built there. For those that are unaware, this vessel actually assisted in the rescue of many terrified passengers from the ice-cold Atlantic Ocean, after the doomed *Titanic* sank on her very first crossing, on 14 April 1912. In 1906, the RMS *Mauretania* was constructed at Swan Hunter and, in more recent times, the world-famous HMS *Ark Royal* was built there as well. The banks of the Tyne at Wallsend were once festooned with magnificent shipyard cranes, making Tyneside's industrial skyline just as awe-inspiring as any other, but, in 2008, work began to dismantle them. Still, the legacy of Swan Hunter and North East shipbuilding lives on, though a gaunt, vacant emptiness is left behind in its wake, where the one-time

The River Tyne, as seen from my old garden in St Anthony's Estate.

king of North East industrialisation once stood. Quite an impressive addition to the curriculum vitae of the area one might think, but Tyneside has more…

Although Newcastle upon Tyne had always been a key area – occupied by the Romans 2,000 years ago and used as a primary market town from the Middle Ages onwards – the development and progression of Newcastle and Tyneside, as a whole, was, of course, largely down to coal and its distribution. It was North East coalmining that put Tyneside on the map for good. Tyneside coal was mined and then shipped throughout the rest of the UK and beyond.

Tyneside is also known for a great deal of other things too: the remains of Hadrian's Wall, the one-time magnificent Roman structure that ran eighty Roman miles (seventy-five of our modern miles) across the top of England, ending in Tyneside; railway pioneer George Stephenson, born in close proximity to Tyneside (Wylam in Northumberland); the world's biggest half marathon; the world-famous bridges that span the River Tyne; and one of the finest ales on the planet – Newcastle Brown Ale.

I might also go on to say that TV classics such as *The Likely Lads* and *Auf Wiedersehen Pet* were filmed here in Tyneside, along with action movies *Stormy Monday*, starring Tommy Lee Jones and Melanie Griffith, and *Get Carter*, staring Sir Michael Caine. Celebrities are also in abundance here in

Tyneside, including Ant and Dec, Sir Bobby Robson, Alan Shearer, Cheryl Cole (*née* Tweedy), Robson Green, Sting, Catherine Cookson, William T. Stead, Mark Knopfler, Neil Tennant, Sir Ridley Scott, Hank Marvin, Sharon Percy, and not forgetting Brian Johnson from the rock legends AC/DC. The list goes on and on, giving Tyneside so much to be proud of.

And so onto the paranormal aspect of Tyneside. Did you know, for example, that Tyneside is home to one of the world's most famous haunted houses? The haunting of Willington Mill, in North Tyneside, occurred between 1835 and 1847 and caused much debate throughout the paranormal fraternity back in its heyday. It went on to become one of the best-attested and most authenticated cases anyone had ever recorded. And what about the Marsden Grotto pub in South Shields, which was once known as 'Britain's most haunted pub'? Furthermore, one of the world's most terrifying cases of poltergeist infestations, subsequently endorsed by Alan Murdie of the Society for Psychical Research as 'one of the most significant cases in the last fifty years', took place in South Tyneside during late 2005 and almost the duration of 2006. More on these cases later, however.

In recent years, Tyneside has become rather well known for its 'paranormal hotspots'. Don't get me wrong, prior to these recent times, there was not a lack of ghosts and hauntings in our region; on the contrary, these places, and the ghosts that are attached to them, have most certainly always been there. But ever since TV programmes began jumping on the ghost-hunting entertainment bandwagon, the world, it seems, has been bitten by the 'ghost-hunting bug'. I am glad to say that my passion for the paranormal stems back to my earliest experiences as a boy growing up on Tyneside, prior to all the programmes now showing.

A book on Tyneside's ghosts has been a long time coming. Of course, it must be borne in mind that to detail every single ghostly account in this region, within these pages, would be an enormous task – indeed, nigh on impossible – so, quite frankly, I didn't attempt to. What I did set out to achieve was to document a substantial collection of chilling ghost stories that differ from any other work on ghosts in our region to date. By that I mean including many accounts that are, quite simply, not the same old tales, although, admittedly, there are one or two accounts that have been re-written and freshened up for a whole new batch of readers. I think that in this respect my goal has been accomplished. I hope you will agree.

I have been involved in ghost-lore and paranormal investigation for most of my adult life, so a lot of these local tales, of headless horseman, phantoms, spectral Grey Ladies and such like, were, of course, already known to me. All I had to do was write them up. However, there is a myriad of supernatural tales in this book that have been rescued from the brink, after almost being forgotten forever in the sands of time. To resurrect these tales in their finest detail and in their original form has been an absolute privilege and, of course, in doing so it gives a whole new generation – and future generations for that matter – the chance to read and learn about our phantom friends for themselves. Other stories have been hitherto undiscovered and, I am pleased to

Gone but not forgotten. Old cranes line the banks of the former shipyard that was Swan Hunter. In the foreground, you can see the remains of the Roman fort, Segedunum, from which Wallsend gets its name. (Courtesy of Walter Ritson)

Another Swan Hunter crane towers over the Ship Inn pub in Wallsend. (Courtesy of Walter Ritson)

say, are now being told in this volume for the very first time.

So, we have a well-mixed and overabundant volume of Tyneside's finest and most chilling ghosts. But, of course, I wouldn't expect anything less; you see, the North East, in my opinion, has always been one of the most haunted areas in the UK. With a rich history and a turbulent past, the northern districts and borderlands were laid siege to by the Scots and English for many years. The battles and killings that took place there must have numbered into the thousands. The land is now forever soaked in blood, and it is not hard to imagine the pain and anguish that these combatants and prisoners must have felt in their final days. They do say traumatic events can somehow be recorded into the fabric of stone buildings and, of course, the surrounding earth. If this is so, I dare say you will find a ghost lurking in just about every corner.

It was only in the 1980s and '90s that people started investigating our wonderful North East haunted heritage in detail, unearthing a wealth of denizens from the past in the most usual of places. I personally have discovered a wide range of hauntings during my years of research, and I dare say I will find more. Other well-respected and thorough ghost hunters will undoubtedly find more too. This is why the book can not cover every ghost in the region. People are passing into the next world all the time, and different aspects of our past are forever coming back to literally haunt us, so it is without doubt that new ghosts will ultimately be discovered. Who knows, maybe one day we will even find out the answers we are so desperately seeking.

This book is not a scientific treatment, nor is it a tool to prove to readers that ghosts do exist. I feel there is sufficient literature out there, if one is prepared to find it, which already proves the existence of ghosts and poltergeists. This is a book to sit down with in your favourite armchair, perhaps on a stormy night or on a cold winter's day, or whenever the mood takes you. Whether you believe in the supernatural or not, the important thing is that you take pleasure in meandering slowly through these pages, learning for yourself the wondrous ghostly tales and folkloric legends of Tyneside's haunted heritage.

Darren W. Ritson, 2011

A view of Newcastle from Byker, Tyneside (c. 1970). (Courtesy of Walter Ritson)

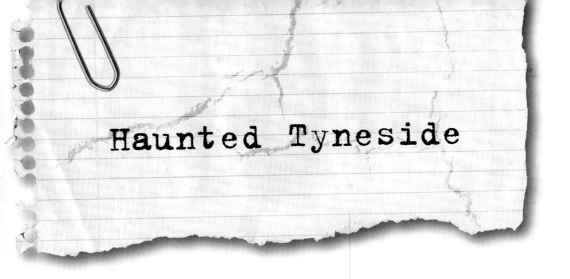

Haunted Tyneside

Souter Lighthouse, South Shields

A few years ago I took part in a radio show and the topic of conversation was ghosts. During the course of the show, we began chatting about haunted headlands and old, disused lighthouses, and why they could be potential locations for hauntings. On air, we discussed the most famously haunted lighthouse within the Tyneside region, which is of course Souter Lighthouse in South Shields. It was opened in 1871 and is now in the ownership of the National Trust.

The ghosts that reside there are said to be that of the former lighthouse keeper, a woman named Isabella, who was related to the famous North East heroine Grace Darling, and a bad-tempered spirit said to be that of a colliery worker from a nearby miners' village. Staff had reported odd goings-on for a while, including the opening and closing of doors and the sound of footsteps in empty corridors.

In recent years, after the *Most Haunted* TV programme recorded an episode there during its first series, paranormal groups

Souter Lighthouse in South Tyneside, said to be haunted by a former lighthouse keeper. The shade of a woman called Isabella, a relation of the North East heroine Grace Darling, has also been spotted here, allegedly.

have since been in to investigate its claims of ghostly activity, and they have all testified to it being a genuinely haunted location. I have not had the opportunity of spending a night there yet, but had I been given the chance to by the aforementioned 'amateur ghost-busters', I would have politely declined their offer.

I have visited the lighthouse on many occasions without experiencing one iota of paranormal activity. That's not to say it isn't haunted though; on the contrary, I believe it may well be. There is enough witness testimony out there to support the notion that the lighthouse is haunted.

The Marsden Grotto, South Shields

The Marsden Grotto pub is thought, by some, to be the most haunted pub in Britain. It is situated in the limestone cliffs of South Shields in Marsden Bay, along the North East coast of England, and sits on beach level. Due to occasional freak high tides from the North Sea, it has been known to flood. It stands opposite the famous Marsden Rock, and its history dates back well over 200 years.

The Marsden Grotto was built in 1782 by a lead miner from Allenheads called Jack Bates, who found himself out of work and came to the area in search of employment. After he subsequently found the caves in the cliff face, he blasted them into what we see today with his explosives. This is why he is known historically as Jack the Blaster. He and his wife Jessie lived in the home they had made for the next ten years, until Jack's death in 1792. The cave dwellings were left

derelict and not fit to live in until around 1826, when a local man called Peter Allan renovated the dilapidated establishment and made it fit for human habitation once more. He named it the Tam O'Shanter, but it was soon renamed the Marsden Grotto. During Peter Allan's time there, the smugglers of the day would often frequent the area and, more particularly, this stretch of coastline. They became very friendly with Mr Allan, and often used his caves as a hideaway for themselves and for their ill-gotten gains and contraband.

Legend has it that in the 1840s, a local HM customs and revenue man, who was out to catch these vagabonds, made friends with a young and inexperienced smuggler. The smuggler soon cottoned on to what was going on and a fight ensued between the two. This resulted in the young rogue being shot and killed by the customs man. The smugglers' tankard that he used during his drinking sessions in the old alehouse was nailed up on the wall in the caves. It is said that if any man drinks from the smugglers' tankard, he would be forever cursed. It was also believed by the locals that should anyone move the tankard from the wall, the establishment would also be psychically disturbed and the restless spirit of the young smuggler would return to disrupt any peace.

It was from this point on that the Grotto began to experience ghostly goings-on and alleged paranormal activity. Objects would move around by themselves; dark shadows were seen to flit around in the even darker caves; and local legend has it that the smugglers' tankard, when left on the bar at night with ale in, would mysteriously be empty in the morning.

The Marsden Grotto pub; once named the most haunted pub in Britain.

The original smugglers' tankard. Sadly, the tankard was stolen from the pub many years ago. Could this be the cause of all the unrest? (Courtesy of Michael J. Hallowell, Thunderbird Craft and Media)

Some say it is the smuggler returning from the grave to drink his favourite ale from his favourite tankard. It is also said that on stormy nights, you can hear the screams of the tormented souls of the smugglers who died in the caves; those who lost their lives by either drowning in the freak high tides or being viciously murdered by their so-called comrades.

In late 2004, I was fortunate enough to have been able to fully investigate the premises from top to bottom. The manageress at the time, Sue Birkbeck, seemed genuinely concerned (and interested) in what was going on at her new pub. She had experienced a whole host of odd paranormal phenomena since moving into the property, and, after finding out about the pub's 'most haunted' reputation, decided to call in our team to shed some light on the matter.

On the nights of 19 November and 17 December 2004, we conducted some overnight research to see if we could witness any paranormal activity. The nights in question proved very interesting, to say the least, with a whole range of occurrences documented. Unexplained footsteps were heard in areas where nobody was around, lights turned themselves on and off for no reason whatsoever, but the strangest thing of all was when all present – about fifteen investigators and the pub manageress – were sitting in the cave bar in total darkness and in silence at around 4 a.m. From out of nowhere, we all heard the unmistakable sound of a party. Murmuring was heard coming from close by, along with the clinking and chinking of wine glasses. It was like the sound from a function, or a gathering of people. But it couldn't have been, because there was no party going on anywhere nearby at that time.

I actually suggested it might have been the noise from a party being held elsewhere in the area, with the wind carrying the sound gently down the coastline. But we all went outside and listened out for it – silence. If it was from outside, then why could we only hear it inside and in the main area of the building, where functions would normally have taken place? To this day, the events of those nights still remain a mystery, and one can only presume we all heard – and don't forget there was over fifteen of us – the ghostly echoes of a party that once took place there.

In fact, these two investigations were so compelling that they were eventually written up and discussed in Jeff Belanger's book *Encyclopaedia of Haunted Places, Ghostly Locales from around the World*. Jeff had contacted an old friend of mine, Paul Roberts, founder of the UK TAPS team, which assisted in the investigations, and Paul then relayed our results to him for the book.

More recently, in April 2010, I was asked to help out on an investigation atthe pub with Northumberland-based researcher John Triplow. During the course of this investigation, I was fortunate enough to have seen the 'ghost cat' flitting around the pub. Many people have seen this cat over the years, and in actual fact, out of all the ghosts that are said to reside at the Grotto, it is the most frequently seen. My sighting is just another in a string of many already documented, and I dare say by the time you have read this, the chances are that he will have been seen yet again.

The Railway Inn, South Shields

According to legend, the Railway Inn was once managed by an elderly lady who had quite a forceful disposition. Even in these relatively sedate times it takes strength of character to manage a riverside tavern. Back then it was even harder. Nevertheless, she kept an orderly house and ensured that the pub was a pleasant watering hole for those in need of refreshment. At some point gentle hints were made that she should perhaps be thinking of hanging her

drying towel over the pumps for one last time. But the old dear would have none of it. The Railway Inn was her home, and she fully intended to stay there till the day she died.

Despite her failing health, the landlady struggled on until things became impossible. However, out of respect for her wishes, she was allowed to stay on the premises until she died. After her death, there was a short period during which there was no paranormal activity whatsoever. But then, it

The Railway Inn at South Shields (now The Waterfront) is reputed to be 'well haunted'.

seems, the old lady decided that she wasn't going to leave her old home after all. Before long, drinkers at the tavern began to catch fleeting glimpses of her at the bar area.

Whatever you perceive ghosts to be, it is certainly true that they exhibit many of the characteristics of their flesh-and-blood alter-egos. In life, the old lady of the Railway Inn was not averse to tugging the hair of any of the bar staff she was displeased with. A friend of Mike Hallowell (Alan Tedder) spoke with a barmaid from the pub several years ago. She told him that on more than one occasion, she had felt her hair being sharply tugged by an invisible hand. Perhaps she wasn't doing things to the old lady's liking!

Actually, the phenomenon of hair-pulling is common in hauntings that display poltergeist-like activity. Shoulder tapping is also regularly reported. Also at the Railway Inn, a joiner was doing some maintenance work in the bar when an icy blast of wind shot across the room and froze him to the bone. He angrily shouted, 'For goodness sake, shut that door!' and then turned around to find that the door was shut and that there was no one else in the vicinity.

The South Shields Poltergeist

Sitting at work one day, my (then) line manager came up to me and uttered the words, 'My friend's daughter has a ghost.' This is probably one of the best things that someone has ever said to me – except for, 'Congratulations, it's a girl', of course – and with those six words, came one of the greatest cases of poltergeist infestation and documentation I have ever come across. I

didn't know it at the time, but from that point on my life was to change forever, and in more ways than one.

Every respectable paranormal investigator dreams of the big case; this was my big case. In fact, it turned out to be so big that it has recently been endorsed by Alan Murdie, the head of the Spontaneous Cases Committee for the Society for Psychical Research, as 'one of the most significant cases of poltergeist activity in the last fifty years'. Others have labelled it the 'next Enfield', with some saying it is 'the poltergeist case of the century'. Legendary author, paranormal investigator and philosopher Colin Wilson regards the weighty tome that was written about the entire affair as 'one of the great classic works on the poltergeist', and Guy Lyon Playfair, who investigated the infamous Enfield Poltergeist case with the late Maurice Grosse back in 1977–8, said, 'This book is a welcome addition to the literature on one of the most bewildering phenomena we are ever likely to come across.' I guess at the end of the day, we must have done something right.

Of course, when I say 'we', I also refer to my fellow researcher that is Michael J. Hallowell, for it was his expert services I called upon when I first became aware of the case. Mike has been investigating and writing on the paranormal for best part of forty years, so when it came to choosing my co-investigator for this case, there was really no one else. At the time, however, we had very little idea of what was in stall for us. The family members concerned had informed me that things were occurring in the house that they couldn't explain. Over the space of a few months, I kept in close

Darren W. Ritson (right) and Michael J. Hallowell.
The investigators and authors of best-selling book
The South Shields Poltergeist.

The South Shields Poltergeist, *2nd edition.*

contact with this family and offered advice and support in whatever way I could. At my request, Marianne (the female occupant of the house) kept a diary of the day-to-day occurrences that were taking place: dates, times, what occurred and who witnessed it; everything from that point on would be documented.

Every now and again I would receive a call from Marianne and she would be quite frightened to say the least. I would reassure her and explain to her the theories behind the poltergeist, as by now this is what I had suspected it may have been. From what she had told me previously, it bore the hallmarks of an active 'polt'. One day, while I was sitting at home, I received a call from a friend at work who told me that Marianne had tried to contact me there. I was asked to 'contact her immediately', as she was at her wits end. I subsequently phoned her up and spent the next three to four hours chatting with her on the telephone. She explained that whatever it was had seemed to step up a gear, and was now becoming terrifying for her and her family. 'Enough is enough,' she said, 'I really need you to come over.'

At this point I telephoned Mike Hallowell and told him about the case and what my preliminary thoughts were on it. I had thought to myself that if this lady was speaking the truth, and strange things were really happening in her house, then this case could have been a live polt at work. It all sounded too good to be true, so when I asked Mike if he would accompany me to the house on my first visit, he jumped at the chance.

The day of our first visit arrived and we headed off to Lock Street. We spent a whole afternoon at the house chatting and discussing the alleged events with nothing much happening at all in the way of paranormal phenomena. This occurs rather a lot, with almost 99 per cent of the houses you visit during alleged hauntings producing absolutely nothing when the investigators turn up. I thought this was going to be another one of those occasions, and so did Mike. How wrong we were.

Late afternoon, while standing in Marianne's son's room, we experienced what we later named the 'South Shields Poltergeist' at work. Small toys were thrown around the room with such speed that it was hard to keep up with them. One of them, a small, yellow plastic nut, flew across the room so fast it bounced off the cupboard door and hit Marianne on the backside, giving her quite a sting. A ball appeared from out of nowhere on the young boy's bed and when we touched it, we found it was rather hot! Other toys slid off the shelves and landed in the tin wastebasket, and we recorded a whole host of knocks and raps during a lock-off period in Robert's room. It was bewildering to say the least.

As the days turned into weeks, and the weeks turned into months, the activity at Lock Street got worse and worse: objects were thrown around the house almost on a daily basis; doors that were locked, were later found unlocked; and young Robert complained to Marianne and her partner, Marc, that he could see a man in the house at times. On one occasion, he woke up to see him floating over his bed. Other objects, such as keys, phones, and credit cards were taken from their original places and hidden from the owners. They would often turn up when least expected.

The ball on the bed appeared from nowhere. It landed where you see it and was hot to touch. This was one of the many odd occurrences we witnessed on our first visit to the 'haunted house'. (Darren W. Ritson and Michael J. Hallowell)

One of the more perplexing aspects of the case was when the poltergeist began to materialise and throw money around. Coins would rain down from nowhere and bounce around the house. This occurred in front of Mike and I on a number of occasions, and it also occurred in the presence of two other well-respected investigators from PSI in Swindon – Dave Wood and Nicky Sewell – who I had invited up to observe in the case.

In total, around twenty-five people witnessed the bewildering phenomena at 42 Lock Street between late 2005 and the end of 2006. Most of them provided witness statements for the book that was published about the case, *The South Shields Poltergeist: One Family's Fight Against an Invisible Intruder.*

Of course, there is an old saying that goes, 'Things always get worse before they get better,' and by heck did it get worse. In fact, the polt turned so ferocious, so vicious and so malevolent, I asked myself just what the hell were we really dealing with. It stepped up its campaign of terror by sending death threats and sadistic messages to Marianne via her mobile phone. Messages such as, 'The bitch will die today,' and 'Can get you when you awake and I'll come for

A collection of coins that were thrown by the poltergeist during one afternoon at the 'haunted house' in South Shields. (Darren W. Ritson and Michael J. Hallowell)

you when you're asleep bitch,' give you an idea of some of the evil things it said. The mobile phones were examined and even dismantled at times, yet the text messages kept on coming.

By far the worst aspect of the case was when it decided to inflict injury on Marc. It did this by cutting him. One night, after retiring to bed, he felt a hot, burning sensation on his skin under his t-shirt and when he took off his top to show Marianne, his skin was red. Suddenly, cuts and welts began to slowly appear on his body and, before long, he looked like something from out of a slasher movie. It was as though an assailant had assaulted him with a knife. His torso was in a complete state

and, as you can imagine, total panic ensued. Telephoning Mike at about midnight for help, Marianne frantically explained what had just occurred and pleaded for him to come and help. This he did, arriving at the house some time later.

Later on, and in the presence of Mike, Marc was attacked again by the polt, only this time Mike had his camera at the ready and he filmed it! Our number one motive was to help the family concerned, and then document what we could, and this should be borne in mind. By next morning, however, the cuts and welts on Marc's torso had completely healed up and had vanished altogether. They had appeared paranormally, and had disappeared paranormally

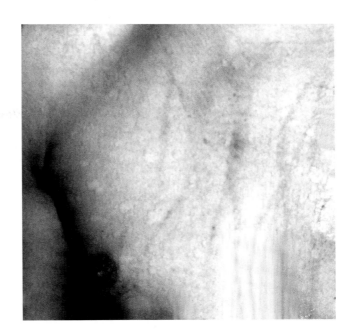

A close-up of some of the cuts and scratches that appeared on Marc's torso. Attacks like these are extremely rare indeed. (Darren W. Ritson and Michael J. Hallowell)

Taken from the actual video footage, this bottle of water was, astonishingly, found balancing on its edge. The bottle was nudged by investigator Michael Hallowell at the time, yet it didn't fall over. (Darren W. Ritson and Michael J. Hallowell)

too. Real cuts like that should have taken a week or so to heal properly, yet these had vanished within the space of hours. Marc was cut by the poltergeist on three or four more occasions and each time was caught on film. On one occasion, he was attacked in front of over ten people, three of which had video cameras and recorded it.

After suffering at the hands of this sadistic entity for almost a year, the poltergeist activity at Lock Street eventually subsided. It had been one hell of a ride for the family concerned, and, of course, Mike and I. Others that had came in to observe what was going on all left the house bewildered, confused and scratching their heads in utter disbelief. The South Shields Poltergeist really put the Lock Street family, and Mike and I, to the test, but in the end we emerged victorious. It had been a long, hard battle against a vicious entity – call it what you will – that would stop at nothing to wreak havoc on those that came within close proximity to it. For Marc, Marianne and Robert, the battle was now over. For Darren and Mike, however, a whole new series of battles were to begin – battles that we are still fighting to this day. But that, my dear reader, is another story completely.

The Red Lady of Cleadon Mill

Researching this book was like researching any other book I have written. By that I mean a total joy. The beauty of discovering new ghost tales, and rediscovering old ones, is that you never know where you are going to end up next; a deserted mental hospital maybe? An underground lead mine, perhaps a 400-year-old hotel or a 700-year-old manor house, even a 1,000-year-old castle? From venue to venue, I go searching for traces of the afterlife or echoes of the past that may be lurking in the dark corners of our wonderfully haunted lands.

Working with Mike Hallowell has been one of the highlights of my ghost-hunting career and it is thanks to him that I have been privileged to hear and learn about many of the North East's finest, most fascinating and, more often than not, long-forgotten ghost stories, with the following account being no exception. During my many visits to Mike's house, I often raid his archives in search of new stories to write about, or to perhaps feature in an upcoming volume. The following story came about in this way.

As most South Tynesiders know, there is an old abandoned mill house on Cleadon Hills in the South Tyneside area. The mill – or rather, what's left of it – has been restored, and is one of the borough's many interesting historical monuments. According to legend, a couple and their daughter once inhabited the mill. The teenager was, by all accounts, stunningly beautiful and had a queue of local farm-hands lining up to court her. Although the young lady could have had her pick of the local lads, to her father's chagrin, she fell madly in love with a young ne'er-do-well who was part of a smuggling gang working in the area. Despite her parent's protestations, the miller's daughter met with her contrabanding beau at every opportunity. Love, it seems, had blinded her to the shadier side of her suitor's lifestyle.

Whenever the opportunity arose, she would don her pretty red dress and engage in secret liaisons with the handsome scallywag, always being careful not to draw her father's attention. But the lad couldn't have been all that bad. He treated the miller's daughter like a princess, showering her with gifts and kisses. None of this impressed her father, however, whose mood darkened with every passing day. At some point, the young smuggler proposed to the miller's daughter, promising to abandon his life of crime and embark upon a respectable career. The girl, determined, told her father of their plans, which was a terrible mistake.

Incandescent with rage, the miller forbade his daughter from leaving the house until she agreed to marry a suitor of better stock. He also ordered her boyfriend not to come anywhere near the premises. Understandably, the young lady was distraught. Unable to see her fiancé, she stopped eating and descended into the depths of depression. In vain, she tried to get her father to recant, but he stubbornly refused. She would marry someone 'respectable' or not at all. Devoid of hope, the miller's daughter decided that she

The ruin of Cleadon Mill on Cleadon Hills, South Tyneside. This is home to the ghost of the Red Lady.

An artistic representation of the spectral Red Lady of Cleadon Hills. She is said to walk here eternally, after she leapt from the top of the mill. (Courtesy of Michael J. Hallowell, Thunderbird Craft and Media)

would rather die than be separated from the only person she truly loved. The next day she approached the mill, ascended, took one last look at the beautiful countryside around her and promptly threw herself to the ground. Sometime later, the miller found his daughter's broken body in a pool of blood. She was wearing the red dress that had so enchanted her boyfriend. What became of the miller, his wife or the daughter's boyfriend we do not know. However, the ghost of the young lady soon began to appear – still wearing the red dress – in and around the mill. She is, apparently, still waiting for her lover to rescue her from the clutches of her possessive father.

A sad tale of lost love wouldn't you agree? And my thanks to Mike Hallowell for allowing me to reproduce his text in this volume. Incidentally, Mike and I took a drive up to Cleadon Mill to photograph it for this book and, in all honesty, we both felt a certain degree of apprehension when we were up there. Mike has visited Cleadon Mill many times prior to our little jaunt and had never felt what he felt on that day. For me, it was my first visit to the mill and I dare say my last. It really felt as though we were being watched during our time there, and we couldn't help thinking something bad would occur if we stayed. With that, I took my pictures, packed away the camera and headed back to the car.

The Albion Inn, Pelaw

The Albion Inn in Pelaw is allegedly haunted by an old and well-liked former customer, known simply as Charlie. Not much is known about this fellow, except the fact he was a fine and upstanding citizen within his community and was identified locally as 'The Gentleman of Bill Quay'. It is said that Charlie passed over in the early 1960s, but no one knows exactly when.

The pub, it seems, is still graced with Charlie's presence, and it appears that death itself could not discourage the 'old fella' from visiting his much-loved drinking den. It wasn't long after his sad departure that numerous witnesses saw his ghost in the bar. A one-time landlady saw him bold as brass standing at the bar. Knowing he was actually dead, she courageously proceeded to approach him, not taking her eyes off him for one second. He subsequently vanished before her eyes.

Another occupant of the pub, the successor of the landlady, admits to having some strange experiences there, but has never seen the shade of old Charlie for himself. He would hear the doors in the pub open and close on their own, often followed by an unnatural 'tap tap tap' noise like that of a walking stick on the wooden floor. Could this have been Charlie? Or perhaps another spectral punter that also wishes to reside there in the afterlife?

As a boy, I used to enjoy many bike rides with my father. During these outings, we used to stop at the Albion for a fizzy orange juice. The inn was approximately half way around our usual cycle route and its location made it a good place to rest for a while. We would leave the bikes outside, while enjoying our refreshing break. My father often told me the ghost stories connected to the pub during our visits there, and on once occasion he even tried to capture the ghost on film with his camera – but to no avail.

Has Charlie been sighted recently? The author cannot say, but one thing is for certain; the character and personality of old Charlie has engraved itself into the fabric of this wonderful old building in a way that its regulars should be thankful for. Interestingly, in the summer of 2009, some colleagues of mine spent a whole night in this pub in search of old Charlie, unfortunately without any success.

The Viking of Boldon

Some time ago, Mike Hallowell received a letter from a *Shields Gazette* reader in Boldon Colliery. She had written to him in response to a previous article in the 'WraithScape' column, regarding a mysterious Viking longship, which was allegedly buried in the vicinity of South Shields town centre.

She told him that back in the 1930s, when her father was a young boy, the remains of another mystery vessel were located in the

River Don near West Boldon. This too was supposedly a Viking longship, although alternative versions of the legend state that the boat was located at the River Don at Jarrow.

Of course, were such remains to be found in Jarrow, the Boldons or any other part of the borough, they would be of inestimable cultural and archaeological value. The interesting thing about the Boldon version of the story, however, is that it ties in nicely with a ghost story related to Mike by yet another reader.

According to this reader, Jim, two miners' wives from Boldon Colliery were 'frightened half to death' one evening when walking beside the Don, or 'the burn' as it is known locally. As they approached a patch of particularly long grass, they were surprised to see a pair of feet sticking out. Assuming that someone may have been hurt, they ran to provide assistance.

To their amazement, they saw that the figure was actually a young man with long blond hair and a beard. His clothes seemed to be made from leather and tweed, and his 'shoes' were actually boots that came half way up his calves. According to Jim, he looked like an 'ancient Briton, or a Viking'.

Within seconds, the women realised that he was badly hurt. There was blood around his mouth, and he was breathing rapidly but shallowly. He was also, apparently, staring directly up into the heavens with a vacant expression and glazed eyes. Both women could see that he was dying.

One of them said that they should run for help, but before they could depart a strange, yellow-white light seemed to engulf the stricken man, and he vanished from sight. Both the witnesses then ran home terrified.

Who was the spectral figure? Could he have been a Norseman, perhaps critically wounded in a fight? Did the women watch a ghostly re-enactment of his last few minutes on earth? Was his fate in some way intertwined with that of the mystery longboat? Who knows.

It is not impossible that a Viking longship could indeed have travelled such a distance inland. Whereas the Don at Boldon is now little more than a stream, in ancient times it was much deeper and broader.

As for the ghostly apparition that frightened the two anonymous ladies all those years ago, I know of nothing to substantiate his existence apart from this one anecdotal tale. That doesn't mean that he never lived, of course.

I must confess that this is the first time I've heard the story of Boldon's ghostly Viking, but I'm sure that there must be other people out there who know something about it.

Opposite, top *The Albion Inn at Pelaw, said to be the haunt of a ghost known as Charlie.*

Opposite, bottom *An interior shot of the Albion Inn; an attempt by my father to catch the ghost known as Charlie on film. (Courtesy of Walter Ritson)*

Above The area in West Boldon where the ghost of a Viking was once seen.

Left An artistic representation of the ghost-Viking thought to haunt the area in South Tyneside known as 'the burn', in West Boldon. (Courtesy of Michael J. Hallowell, Thunderbird Craft and Media)

The Wheatsheaf and the Black Horse, West Boldon

Prior to buying my trusty car, I would have to 'bus it' almost everywhere I went. Every week on a Sunday, I would visit Mike Hallowell's house to crack on with one of our many book manuscripts, work on our website, or just chill out in his wonderful little garden and catch up after a long, hard week at work. The No. 9 service, which ran from Wallsend to Sunderland, would take me through the Tyne Tunnel, through Jarrow and on to the Boldons. As the bus made its way through West Boldon, it took me up Rectory Bank past two extremely haunted pubs that stand opposite one another. Every time we went past them, I longed to go in and visit. I had heard of the pubs' ghosts many years ago and made it my business to one day go in and have a chat with the staff.

We will begin with the Wheatsheaf pub. This old alehouse made news in the *Chronicle* back in 2004, when a visiting psychic picked up on a number of spirit children that were said to be 'trapped there'. The story went on to say that a number of hidden artefacts that belonged to a certain child known as Jessica, were hidden behind a fireplace on the upper levels of the pub. This information was brought forward by the visiting psychic, so when the wall was knocked down and some children's belongings, including a shoe, were found in the aperture, confirming the psychic's testimony, you can imagine the surprise of the staff and the locals alike.

The pub, prior to that point, had, indeed, been subject to odd, ghostly goings-on, with bar glasses being moved around, doors opening and closing on their own, ghostly figures being seen (again on the upper levels of the pub), and objects going missing only to reappear again in a place where the owners would least expect it. By the late 1990s, the pub had gained the reputation of being one of the most haunted pubs in the region; if not *the* most haunted. By 2007, people were being told that over thirty ghosts haunted it, which if you ask me, is unfounded.

I eventually had the chance to spend the night in the pub back in April 2008, and had some rather odd experiences to say the least. The most unusual incident was when fellow investigator Mark Winter recorded what sounded like a young girl's voice saying the words, 'Yes, I am cold, very cold.' These words were recorded in the actual room where the fireplace was dug out, and after an investigator had asked the question, 'Jessica, are you here?' Pretty compelling stuff if you ask me, but not conclusive, however.

We now move across the road and pay a visit to the Black Horse pub. At the time of our visits back in May 2008, it was run by punk-rock legend Pete Zulu (Peter Robson), who was one of the band members of the famous Toy Dolls. The Black Horse was formerly a coaching inn and is said to be one of the North East's oldest pubs. The inn was built around 1642, and rumour persists that it was built upon the site of yet another, older alehouse. It is not known if the earlier building was reputed to be haunted or not, but the present pub most certainly is – at least according to the then owners, Sarah Reid and Peter Robson.

The Wheatsheaf pub in West Boldon; one of the many haunted locals that I have had the privilege of investigating…and with some very interesting results.

I met Peter and his wife a few years ago and interviewed them, as well as some of the bar staff and locals, in regard to the pub's alleged resident spirits. Peter had an interesting tale to tell of an odd incident that occurred in the kitchen area of the pub one night:

I had been preparing some food in the kitchens and used some bowls that one would usually fill with chips as a side dish. I had cleaned them up and put them away on the shelf in the kitchen and then retired to my bed. The next morning I went downstairs and into the kitchen and found a number of these bowls — that I had put up on the shelf the night before — smashed to pieces on the floor about 10ft from the actual shelves they were originally placed on. The strange thing about this was that the dishes had been smashed to smithereens and I had not heard a darn thing during the night. Smashing crockery is very noisy indeed and you would have thought we'd have heard it. The other thing that puzzled me was the fact that these dishes were found quite far away from the shelves. Now, if they had been teetering on the edge of the shelf and had simply fallen, they would have been found at the foot of the shelving unit and not in a pile some distance away.

These are very interesting points, and it's not the first time in an alleged haunted location that the crockery phenomenon has been reported. In the case of the haunting of Borley Rectory, the sound of smashing crockery was heard, yet no crockery was found to be smashed. This incident occurred in the rectory cottage around the time of the First World War (I don't think an actual time was ever pinned down for this occurrence), and was witnessed by Mr and Mrs Edward Cooper, who resided there at that time.

Peter's sister, Jean, also had a frightening experience at the pub one day, while tending to some cleaning duties. As she sprayed an air freshener around the room, she noticed something very strange. She saw that through the faint mist from the spray, she could see the figure of a man wearing old-style clothing. He walked straight through the spray and vanished right in front of her. The aforementioned tales you have just read are first-hand accounts from people that have all lived and worked at the pub. Just how much truth there is in any of the ghost stories at this fine boozer we will never know for sure, but the fact remains that the locals and the proprietors

believe that the pub does indeed house a few ghosts, and I for one think they may be right.

The Black Horse pub, which stands across the road from the Wheatsheaf. A number of paranormal occurrences have been recorded here over the years, which isn't surprising since it has been around since 1642.

Follingsby Lane, near Boldon

The haunting of Follingsby Lane near Boldon, South Tyneside, is a sad one. It begins on a cold January evening in 1909, when a young couple met up and decided to go for a walk along the lane in question, which led all the way to Boldon. It is thought they reached a stretch of the walk known as Hylton Bridge and travelled some distance beyond that. Where they were actually going no one knows, as there was very little else in that vicinity to actually visit; perhaps they were just out for an evening stroll?

Whatever occurred that fateful day, we know Follingsby Lane was soon to become the location for a vile murder. The modern, and more accepted, story these days suggests that for reasons unknown, the young man, who was named Shipley, seemed to snap into a fit of rage, brought on by an argument with his beloved. He proceeded to take out a revolver and emptied it at close range at the defenceless girl, killing her instantly.

Realising his actions would result in his ultimate hanging, he turned the gun on himself and blew his own brains out, falling next to his girlfriend's body. The two corpses lay silently until their discovery later that night.

But evidence dug up by researcher Mike Hallowell suggests that this version of events is 'full of holes and inaccuracies'. If Shipley did not commit the crime, then on that fateful day not one murder took place, but two.

It was alleged at the inquest that the young man's family had a history of mental illness. One family member was said to have shot himself, which is true, but as Mike points out, 'Committing suicide is not automatically a sign of mental illness. Many people kill themselves because they simply don't want to go on living. There is no clinical or written evidence that I know of to suggest that the man was actually mentally ill.' Another family member is said to have thrown himself down a mineshaft, dying when he hit the bottom. 'This is true,' Mike says, 'but what is less well known is that the man suffered terrible brain damage in a pit accident earlier and was mentally impaired – not mentally ill. It was the brain damage that impaired his faculties, not mental illness.'

Yet another family member was said to have attempted to commit suicide and failed, resulting in him spending the rest of his days in the county lunatic asylum at Sedgefield. Mike adds, 'No one knows why he was put in the asylum – but there's no record of it being for attempting suicide.' There is a suggestion in the tale that whatever affliction had gripped the rest of the family (which now looks doubtful), had now suddenly seized Shipley and precipitated both the murder of his girlfriend and his own suicide.

Again, Mike comes back with some hard facts, saying, 'There were only two cases of alleged mental illness in the family – one on the father's side and one on the mother's – both being dubious, and as they weren't related, there is no link between them which makes for a "history" of insanity.'

Regardless of what really happened, the fact remains that something occurred along Follingsby Lane that evening in 1909, and it has left its mark on the surrounding atmosphere. Yes, there were indeed tragic deaths, but it seems that the run up to these killings are not yet fully understood at present,

Follingsby Lane, the scene of a murder in 1909. (Courtesy of Michael J. Hallowell, Thunderbird Craft and Media)

although Mike believes he has shed some new light on this case and what may have actually happened there.

The two corpses are said to have been moved to the Wheatsheaf pub for a designated period of time. It is alleged that the ghosts of the courting couple have been seen at the pub, as well as at the location of the tragedy.

A colleague of Mike's has walked the path known as Follingsby Lane, and states quite clearly, 'In the area where the tragedy took place, an icy atmosphere never seems to dissipate, even in the heat of the summer.' I was also informed that screaming has been heard near Follingsby Lane on 31 January, the anniversary of the tragedy. Numerous other reports suggest that the area is haunted, and maybe, considering what occurred there all those years ago, it is.

Jarrow Hall

Jarrow Hall is a wonderful little Georgian building, tucked away behind a copse of trees, close to the ruins of Bede Monastery in Jarrow, South Tyneside. It is an elegant, Grade II listed building, which once belonged to the monastic estate of Bede and was built in 1785 by local businessman Simon Temple. Simon was a well-known entrepreneur who opened shipyards in South Shields and Jarrow. As well as bringing coal mining on a very large scale to the area, he was also responsible for the refurbishment of another local venue: Hylton Castle in Sunderland. In 1812, Simon went bankrupt and all his businesses folded. He sold Jarrow Hall to two brothers, Thomas and Robert Brown of London. From this

point onwards, the hall began to see a succession of new owners and residents, and one particular resident, in the early 1840s, was a lady called Isabella Chaytor, who was Thomas' daughter-in-law. She was married to Thomas' son, Thomas Drewett Brown, and the couple moved in after the London brothers had moved out in 1841. Isabella is said to be the resident ghost that walks the upper floors of the building, although she is most frequently seen in the Oval Room.

In more recent years, Jarrow Hall has been used for a number of purposes, including a fever hospital, a nursery school, an ammunition store – where locals were able to get gas masks during the Second World War – and a general store facility, before it was left to fall into disrepair in the late 1960s. In the early 1970s, it was refurbished and made habitable once more, and after final refurbishment work was carried out on the building in 1999, it was restored to its original state. It is currently owned by the Bede Monastery Museum. Inside, mounted upon the walls, is a display entitled 'The Life and Times of Jarrow Hall', which, essentially, is a detailed story about the hall and all its former residents. The place is well worth a visit. I came across this building quite by chance a few years ago, when I was out cycling on my bike, and couldn't resist popping in for a quick chat.

After locking my bike up outside, I made my way into the downstairs café area and, once settled, I asked the waitress if the hall had any ghosts. She told me, ever so enthusiastically, 'Indeed it has!' She then went on to tell me about the odd occurrences that she, and other staff members, had experienced while working in Jarrow Hall. I was told that on occasion, things would

Jarrow Hall, near Bede Monastery, is reputedly haunted by the ghost of Isabella Chaytor, who has been seen standing halfway up the stairs. She has also been observed staring out of the window in the Oval Room on the upper level of the building.

be moved around in the kitchens, such as knives, ladles and other utensils. I asked her if she could have been mistaken, perhaps even fooled, but she alleged that these things would be moved when no one else was in the kitchen area and, on occasions, after she had gotten them out to use. Then the ghost of Isabella Chaytor came up, and the waitress had more to add:

> She is said to haunt upstairs. Sometimes she can be heard as she walks across the floors upstairs. No one is up there at the time and its quite eerie to say the least. I have heard them myself. I have not seen her personally, but there are some people who have. Sometimes on the stairs, halfway up, but most people who see her claim she stands and stares from the window in the Oval Room upstairs.

After chatting with this member of staff, I had a meander upstairs and took a good look around. I later asked if it would be possible to spend a night at the hall, in search of Isabella's ghost, but, sadly, I was told by the Trust that owns the hall that their ghosts should be left alone.

Why does Isabella haunt the building? There is no reason, other than the possibility that she simply liked the hall so much she did not want to leave it. A cliché, I know, but on the whole quite probable.

The Robin Hood pub in Jarrow.

The Robin Hood, Jarrow

The Robin Hood at Primrose Hill, Jarrow, has a long and interesting history. In November 2008, Mike Hallowell visited the pub to interview the proprietor, Jess McConnell, who had an interesting tale to tell.

Apparently, only a day or two prior to Mike's visit, the staff at the pub had experienced a rather odd happening, which they could only describe as 'paranormal'. Not long after closing time, they had tidied up the place and were getting ready to leave for the night, when they heard a loud crashing noise, as if something large had been thrown on to the floor. When they went to find out what the noise was, they were perturbed to discover that a large ornamental clock, which had been fastened quite securely to the wall, had somehow unhitched itself from its fastenings and thrown itself some 10ft across the room. This bemused the staff somewhat, but they thought nothing more of it after picking up the clock, and its many pieces, and placing it on the bar for the night.

Nothing more was said about the incident until a few nights later, when, in front of two burly workmen, the clock decided to launch itself off the wall again. This time, the workmen picked up the pieces and fixed the clock back on to the pub wall. I asked Mike what the workmen had told him, knowing he had been to see them during his visit there. He revealed:

> When I spoke to the two workmen they seemed the honest sort; straight talking, level-headed kind of guys, so I had no reason to think they were not telling the truth. They told me that it was a strange thing to bear witness to and [they] didn't expect it in the least. They also told me that on both occasions, the wooden back of the clock was still left hanging on the wall, whilst the rest of the apparatus had seemingly sauntered through the ether to its final resting place.

Very odd to say the least. The fact that paranormal activity had only recently begun at the pub is no mystery however. It's a well-known fact within ghost-lore that when renovations are taking place in certain properties – as was the case at the time of the clock incidents – the resident ghosts often object. The theory goes that they may not like the changes to the place they know and love so well. For this reason, they simply 'kick off', making their feelings known. I think this is the case here. It would be interesting to find out just who the angry ghost is, and why he/she is venting anger at Jess, the owner. Steps are currently being taken to arrange overnight access to the pub by a colleague of mine. If he is successful, then rest assured, I will be there with him when the doors are locked for the night. If there is a ghost in there we may just find it, and perhaps we will get to the bottom of the mystery. Watch this space...

The haunted clock at the Robin Hood pub in Jarrow. Mysteriously, every now and again, the clock leaps off the wall of its own volition and breaks into pieces upon hitting the floor. (Courtesy of Michael J. Hallowell, Thunderbird Craft and Media)

Angel View Inn, Gateshead

The Angel View Inn is one of the North's finest hotels. It stands across from Sir Anthony Gormley's Angel of the North and was originally built as a farmhouse with stables. Today it serves as a twenty-seven bedroomed hotel, restaurant and conference centre. When one visits the Angel View Inn, the old and original brickwork gives you an idea of how the building may have looked in its earlier days. An old pulley mechanism, attached to the building, has obviously stood the test of time. It was once used for hauling the bales of hay into the former hayloft.

The inn really is a delightful old establishment, and it seems that a couple of its former tenants simply do not want to leave the building. Legend has it that many years ago, a girl was accidentally killed there, after being kicked in the face by a horse while carrying out her duties in the stables. The ghost, who is known as the 'faceless girl', has been observed as she meanders through the hotel corridors and rooms. Witnesses have described her as being 'a terrifying looking spectre that sends chills down the spine.' Of course, seeing a ghost with no face would scare me somewhat too, I imagine.

The Angel View Inn, Gateshead is haunted by a girl with no face, and an abundance of other ghosts.

Angel of the North, Gateshead

Anthony Gormley's magnificent work of art known as the Angel of the North stands across from the Angel View Inn and was erected in 1998 It has become accepted by Tynesiders as one of the icons of the North. Indeed, many times on my journey home from London, I have seen the 66ft-high statue towering into the North East sky and thought to myself, 'I am home'.

Interestingly, in Rob Kirkup's book *Ghostly Tyne & Wear*, it is suggested the actual Angel itself, or at least the land in which it stands, is haunted by a Second World War Nazi recruitment officer. A number of visitors to the site have claimed to have actually seen the phantom. One wonders where this ghostly account came from and whether the spirit originates from the land the Angel was erected on or possibly the statue itself.

I have photographed the Angel of the North on many occasions, and at dusk too, when the sun sinks nicely behind it, casting an eerie red-orange glow across the sky. This is when the phantom is said to make its appearance; 'most commonly in the twilight, just after the last traces of sunlight have faded beyond the horizon,' as Rob Kirkup puts it. It certainly does make for an interesting ghost tale, but a more niggling question remains unanswered: how is it known that the phantom is a recruitment officer?

Another spectre is said to wonder the same corridors, disappearing into the ether whenever he is approached. There has also been much poltergeist-like activity reported at the inn, with objects being thrown around, doors slamming closed, strange smells, unexplained footfalls being heard, and the kettles in certain rooms boiling for no reason.

Back in 2005, I had the honour of being one of the first paranormal investigators in the region to be allowed overnight access to the premises, in order to investigate its alleged supernatural activity. Although we had a quiet night, with no paranormal activity recorded, it was still a worthwhile exercise. Other teams have investigated the building too, one of them carrying out a whole series of experiments. Their team founder – a respected investigator – once told me that they had experienced very active nights and ascertained startling results. It is curious that this team should be successful, as we experienced no paranormal activity whatsoever.

The Angel of the North, or at least the area around it, is said to be haunted by a Nazi recruitment officer from the Second World War.

The Marquis of Granby, Gateshead

The Marquis of Granby is a quaint old pub located on Streetgate, in Sunniside. It is just a stone's throw from the gaunt ruins of the Ravensworth Castle Estate, where the author has spent a night or two in search of ghosts. The pub stands centrally on one of the earliest wagon-ways in the North East of England, which was created in around 1700. Used as a stop-off for weary travellers, the pub, then known as the Granby Arms, was a welcome retreat for rest and recuperatation.

On an inside wall of the inn can be found the story of its resident ghost, thought to be that of an old woman, who appears inside the pub in various places. On most occasions, however, she is reputedly seen inside one of the bedrooms in the private living quarters. Just about every tenant of the pub since the late 1800s has reportedly seen her, and more than one person witnessed the very first sighting.

For the past few years, Mike Hallowell and I have had the pleasure of addressing the first-year students at Northumbria University, as guest lecturers, after being contacted by the Head of Psychology, Dr Nick Neave. He asked us if we could come in and discuss our work with his students. As part of their course, they are required to complete a module on parapsychology, and Dr Neave thought it would be constructive for his students to speak to seasoned investi-

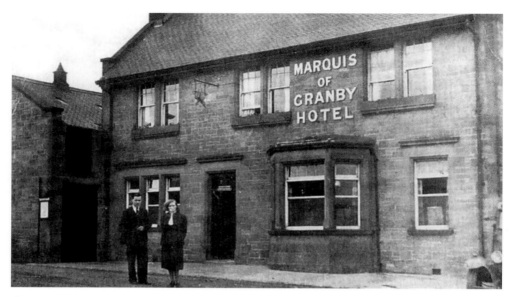

An old image of the Marquis of Granby pub in Sunniside, with my correspondent's (Sheila Gascoigne's) parents standing outside. (Courtesy of Sheila Gascoigne)

gators and well-known authors in the field of paranormal research. Of course, we were delighted to be asked and duly obliged. But what has this to do with the Marquis of Granby? Well, Dr Neave is the chairman of a historical society that holds meetings at the Marquis of Granby on a monthly basis. One of their members is a woman named Sheila, who just happened to have once lived in the Marquis of Granby. When Nick told me this, I was beside myself with joy and wanted to know more about this woman and her family. Nick informed me that back in 2009, she had read the small entry on the pub featured in *Ghost Taverns,* a book by myself and Mike Hallowell, and was surprised to see her pub in there. She had told Nick that although she had not seen anything in the pub in the years that she lived there, which was from 1938–1955, she knew a person that had; a family member. I decided I needed to speak with

Sheila to find out more information and get a reliable account of the ghost of the Marquis of Granby. When I telephoned her, she told me her full name; Sheila Gascoigne (*née* Scorer). She went on to inform me that she was born at the pub and had lived there until she was seventeen years old. The only paranormal encounter she was aware of was experienced by her brother, Arthur. She explained that he and another brother, Gordon, were lying in their beds one night, in 1951, in a room that looked onto the main road, which is now known as Sunniside Road.

A passing lorry swung round a bend in the road and began to climb the short stretch that leads to, and then past, the inn. As the vehicle made its way up the bank, its blazing headlights shone brightly into the brothers' bedroom, illuminating it quite well for a number of seconds. This was when Arthur clearly saw the figure of a dishevelled old woman standing at the foot of the bed, close to the window, with her arms folded. Gordon, at this point, was sound asleep. Within a few short seconds, the room was once more thrust into darkness as the lorry passed by, and when the bedroom light was put on…you've guessed it, no woman could be seen in the room. This is a short but fascinating account; one with an interesting postscript, as we shall soon see.

Sheila and her brother, Arthur, sitting outside the Marquis of Granby, their old family home. It was Arthur who saw the ghost here in 1951. (Courtesy of Sheila Gascoigne)

The area outside the pub is reputed to be haunted too, although I am not too sure where the tale originates. It is thought that a grisly murder took place nearby (perhaps at the pub) in 1865. Although there were suspicions regarding who the perpetrator of the killing was, no one knew for sure the identity of the murderer. It is thought that a local man called Joseph Leybourne was killed after an ongoing feud, which came to a head after a night supping ale in the pub. It is said that Leybourne was bashed around the head with a huge slab of concrete, later found in the undergrowth close to where his body was discovered. It was covered in Leybourne's hair and blood. Some say that this unfortunate fellow haunts the inn and the surrounding area. Interestingly enough, during our conversation on the telephone, Sheila informed me that the ghost her brother Arthur had seen back in 1951, was believed to be the phantom of a distressed mother, in search of her lost son who had gone missing in the mid-1800s. Her son's name; Joseph Leybourne.

The Tudor Rose, Gateshead

A colleague of mine from work once told me of an interesting ghost that resides in his local pub, the Tudor Rose, in Gateshead. Formerly known as the Anchor Inn, this pub is believed to be one of the oldest public houses in the Dunstan area of Gateshead, and when you see it for yourself you can understand why. This ghost story appears (or at least it did when he brought the story to my attention) on the back of the menus placed on every table in the restaurant and bar. It is there for the visitor to read and relish in, while at the same time enjoying the fine cask ales and old-world beers sold at this wonderful pub.

It is said that many years ago, the land in and around the inn was used by the local shipping industry. Being not far from the Dunstan Staiths, there are a few visual reminders of what times were like back then in those 'good old days'. Many people would come and go, so it is not hard to imagine all the drinking that must have gone on when sailors, and the like, would come ashore and frequent the local taverns and inns. Of course, prostitution was rife, and drunken riots and bar-room brawls occurred on a nightly basis. Not a pleasant place for a respectable citizen to 'hang out', so to speak. Indeed, it is from this period that the inn's resident ghost is said to have originated, after being killed – allegedly of course – in one of these nightly skirmishes.

Considering the circumstances of his death, you will be surprised to learn that this ghost, who the locals have nicknamed 'Old George' (which, coincidentally, is also the name of Newcastle's most famously haunted pub), is a rather friendly sort. Having been seen on many occasions, 'Old George' is now regarded as just another regular at the pub. To see if this is true, Mike Hallowell and I set off for an afternoon's drinking in the pub to see if George would make his appearance. Armed with a camera and a wallet full of money, we took our seats in the bar and waited.

The Tudor Rose pub in Dunstan. This old drinking den is famous for its resident ghost, known locally as 'Old George'.

We drank a beer and waited…nothing. Another beer, more waiting…still nothing. By the end of the stint we must have drank six or seven pints, and we thoroughly enjoyed the robust meal we were given by the warm and welcoming staff. Not the usual vigil conditions we adhere to, but this was an unusual ghost hunt; you see, the ghost of 'Old George' is said to appear when the pub is in full swing, and that is why so many people have seen him. Well, except Mike and I, for he made no appearance that day. You never know though, he may just show up on a future visit, as, undoubtedly, we will return in an effort to catch a glimpse of this well-known pub ghost.

Central Arcade, Newcastle upon Tyne

The Central Arcade in Newcastle city centre is a well-known haunted location.

Built in 1838 by Richard Grainger, this elegant building was originally designed as a corn market, but, due to unforeseen circumstances, was used for other purposes instead, until it tragically burned down in around 1868. When it was rebuilt, it was used as a concert hall and art gallery but, due to low attendances, it was sadly closed down.

They say lightning doesn't strike twice in the same place, but in 1901 the building was yet again gutted by a fire, one that almost razed the building to the ground. Yet again it was rebuilt and, in 1906, it opened as one of the finest internally decorated shopping malls the North has ever seen. With wonderful Victorian architecture stretching almost 100ft high, along with a magnificent mosaic floor that looks as though it could have been crafted by the Romans, the Central Arcade (or Windows Arcade as it is also known) stands proud to this day, just as it was when it was rebuilt for the third time in the early 1900s.

J.G. Windows is a music store occupying a large section of the arcade area. It was once the site of a hotel known as the Central Exchange Hotel. Although the fire in 1901 destroyed large parts of Central Arcade, the hotel survived and it is here, at what is now the Windows music store, that an outbreak of poltergeist activity occurred. Footsteps

Central Arcade in Newcastle was built in 1838 by Richard Grainger, and is renowned for being haunted.

were heard coming down a former flight of stairs – one that doesn't exist any more – along with more phantom footfalls on a flight of stairs that does still exist. On one occasion, something brushed passed a member of staff on this stairwell – which leads to the cellar shop – where most of the activity occurred.

Other phenomena were experienced too, with people reporting the feeling of being touched and pushed around by an unseen presence. Objects moved around without any human intervention, and some very startling things were seen first-hand by the staff. A clock was said to have flown off the wall in front of some bemused staff, and on another occasion a shadowy figure was observed moving across the corridor next to the staffroom.

Although it seems to be a clear-cut case of a pesky polt at J.G. Windows, other sections of the arcade have also laid claim to ghostly activity. In a section that was once said to be a tax office, reports came in of a phantom woman seen wearing servants' clothing. She is said to have walked through the wall on one occasion, sending chills down the spines of those that saw it. Thought to be a serving lady who once worked at the nearby hotel; apparently, after finding out she was expecting, she hurled herself down the unused lift shaft that once stood in the arcade.

El Coto Restaurant, Newcastle upon Tyne

Situated in the centre of Newcastle upon Tyne, at 21 Leazes Park Road, is the wonderful Spanish restaurant El Coto. Reports of ghostly goings-on occurring there reached me via one of the owner's sisters, Maxine Gardner, who just happened to be one of my colleagues at work. She approached me while I was at my desk, and told me that the restaurant in question was plagued with paranormal happenings.

Being very much intrigued, and not wanting to let a potential haunting go by undocumented, I asked Maxine if I could contact her sister, Joanne, to hear more, first-hand, about the restaurant's spooky tales. Maxine put me in touch with her sister, and I made the arrangements to go and see her in the restaurant. Before venturing down there, I decided to research the area and the premises where the restaurant stands, and found out some very interesting information. The restaurant, or at least the building that it is housed in, has a rich and varied history that dates back to at least 1811. A whole range of individuals have worked and lived at the location.

The restaurant itself is in an area known as Gallowgate, but contrary to what most people think, the actual gallows of Newcastle stood elsewhere; on the site of the BBC studios on Barrack Road to be precise. The word Gallowgate derives from two words; gallows and gate (the gate to the gallows). Although there were no official executions in this particular area, there are rumours that unofficial hangings took place on Leazes Park Road, at No. 21. These hangings occurred specifically in

The El Coto restaurant in Newcastle city centre, where many strange things have occurred. The owners and staff have been left very much bewildered.

the adjacent courtyard, with one believed to have been carried out in front of the actual building.

Were these hangings meted out to criminals, or were they simply acts of murder; perhaps even suicide? No one knows for sure. One thing is certain; this particular establishment has seen many people come and go, with a host of tradesman and industry folk earning a living there, including solicitors, cabinet makers, insurance agents, joiners, a greengrocer, a sofa manufacturer, and even a gunsmith. Now, of course, it is a successful, thriving city-centre restaurant, only with some of its historic past coming back to haunt it, literally. It's not surprising really when you consider its history.

I remember calling in for the first time and meeting the co-owner, Joanne. She showed me around the restaurant, which is a considerable size I might add, after making me a cup of tea and sharing her ghost accounts. We must have talked for about two and a half hours that afternoon. During the course of my time there, I managed to grab some conversations with her bar staff and waitresses too. They had stories to tell as well, so it seemed pretty clear to me that these people genuinely believed the location to be haunted…but by who, or what, they didn't know.

I was informed that many strange occurrences have taken place at the restaurant, including the sightings of a number of dark shadows seen by Joanne and a few of her staff members. These figures seemed quite solid, she told me, but were only seen from the corner of the eye. This is known as 'corner of the eye syndrome', and sceptics claim it is nothing more than an optical trick. Others suggest that this is the only way to see ghosts! I believe that they can be seen by looking at them straight on, as well as through the peripheral vision.

Mysterious knocks and tapping noises were also heard quite a lot by staff and visitors. These strange 'taps' were usually heard coming from a long corridor that leads to the restaurant area at the back of the building, when there is nobody in that area to make the sound. 'It's as though someone was knocking on the windows, as if they were knocking to come in,' Joanne said. She then went on to tell me about the unexplained footfalls that are often heard coming from empty rooms, but most chilling of all was an account from one of her restaurant staff.

A trigger object and a dictation device were left on the bar during my investigations. This trigger object actually moved on its own in a 'controlled area'.

On one occasion, not long before my visit, the staff member concerned had chores to attend to in the upper section of the restaurant, so he made his way up there, alone. As he approached the top of the stairs, he suddenly felt he was not alone anymore. Suddenly, he heard a voice coming from behind him and, when he turned to see who was there, he was horrified to find he was still on his own. He was the only member of staff in that section of the building at this particular time, and by all accounts he was scared out of his wits.

After hearing all about their alleged resident ghosts, I arranged with Joanne a series of vigils, where I would bring in a team of dedicated paranormal investigators to see if we could document, for ourselves, some of the strange activity. Over the space of two months, we observed the restaurant on numerous occasions and, each time, we all experienced odd phenomena that could not be explained. In one case, a faint mist was filmed in the cellar of the property, and unexplained knocks and bumps came from the areas that Joanne had reported hearing them previously.

On another occasion, we managed to document the movement of an object. A dictation machine, which we had left on a counter, was moved about four or five inches from where it was originally placed. Not only that, it had turned around and was facing the opposite direction to how

The corridor in El Coto, where our motion sensors were tripped by an invisible presence.

we had left it! Investigators were actually sitting in the same room, and only a few yards from it, when this occurred. Finally, a set of motion sensors were tripped when no one was near them. Mark Winter, a friend of mine, was standing in the corridor looking down towards the sensors when they were mysteriously activated. His face was a picture! Another thing to mention is that the founder of another North East-based research team was also present on the investigation, and had brought along his data logger. A data logger is a small electronic device that records room temperatures and relative humidity over a designated period of time. It can also record solar radiation and even wind speed. Graphs and charts can be produced showing the results of the accumulated data; it is a very good piece of equipment for the paranormal investigator. It was noted by this investigator that at the same time the motion sensors were tripped, there was a significant drop in the room's temperature, indicating that something very odd was going on. This is scientific proof that there was a drop in temperature in a place where there shouldn't have been.

Testimony from my accompanying investigators matched the witness reports from Joanne and the staff. I had not informed anyone of what had been reported in the restaurant prior to the visit (this makes my enquiries more interesting), and I only explained what had been going on after the investigations. The staff at the property, combined with the team that investigated it, takes the number of witnesses to over fifteen in total, suggesting that paranormal phenomena is, indeed, occurring at the beautiful city-centre restaurant.

Theatre Royal, Newcastle upon Tyne

A book covering the ghosts of Tyneside would not be complete without a mention of the Grade I listed Theatre Royal on Grey Street, in Newcastle upon Tyne. This beautiful theatre was designed by the famous architects John and Benjamin Green, for Richard Grainger (1797–1861), and was opened in 1837. Tragedy struck, however, in 1889 (some say 1899), when a raging inferno tore through the building and damaged much of the original interior. It was subsequently rebuilt by Frank Mactham (1854–1920) and re-opened once more to the public in 1901. The first ghost story attached to the theatre, however, goes back to the 1880s, when a female theatregoer developed an infatuation with one of the handsome young actors performing there at the time. Although the woman didn't have much money, she made efforts to visit the theatre as many times as she could afford, simply to see the actor she so desired. On one of those occasions, from across the room, the eyes of the actor and the woman eventually met, and a smile was exchanged between them. She decided to wait for her man at the theatre doors and catch him as he was leaving the building. She felt confident that the love she had for him would be reciprocated.

After meeting up with one another they eventually became lovers. After a while, news got out of the affair between the two and, because she was poor and he was a well-to-do actor, the relationship was frowned upon by the majority of folk. They decided that after his final performance at the theatre, they would meet up and elope

The Theatre Royal in Newcastle is home to a number of ghosts, but none more famous than the ghost of a theatre-goer who killed herself after being dumped by an actor she loved dearly.

to get married. But things were to take a horrible turn for the lady, who so desperately loved her man. After the penultimate performance, the actor came clean to his devoted fan and explained to her that he was already married; his heart belonged to another woman. He had only been with her to pass the time and satisfy his own needs.

Devastated by this news, the heartbroken lady went to his final performance and took a seat up in the 'gods', whereupon, after the performance, she threw herself off the balcony and ended her own life. Some folk suggest she may have leaned across the balcony to reach out to the man she could never have, as if to touch him, and fell to her death by accident. It was not long after this event that a faint figure of a woman was seen inside the theatre. Some have observed her carrying a lit candle, while others say she sits forlorn in her seat on the balcony from which she fell. Unfortunately, no one seems to have seen this ghost for many years now. She has no name, and has not been identified in any way. This makes me wonder if the story is anything more than a romantic work of fiction. I guess, until she is seen again by reliable witnesses, we will never know if she exists or not.

There is, however, another ghost story I recently heard that holds a lot more validity. The account came from a reliable source, who wished to remain anonymous. The witness is a member of staff at the theatre, and it was from this individual's partner that I gleaned the story.

I was informed that this particular spectre is seen so frequently, he is becoming very well known to some of the staff. In fact, amazingly, the ghost is seen so much that when members of staff notice him, they often say 'hello'. What is more amazing still, is that as they pass him in the corridor, he often returns the 'hello' and gestures to them with a tip of his hat. The phantom, said to be dressed in Victorian clothes with a black top hat, has, on occasions, even acknowledged certain members of staff by their actual names! Pretty impressive stuff, if you accept the account as true.

The Journal Tyne Theatre, Newcastle upon Tyne

The Journal Tyne Theatre has reputedly been haunted for many years now. The spectre that is said to reside there is known as Robert Courtenedge (some say Crowther), otherwise called 'unfortunate Bob', or 'unlucky Bob'. Unfortunate is an understatement, as you will soon realise when you read how poor old Robert met his demise.

I first went to the Journal Tyne Theatre on a school trip, way back in the late 1970s, and it was during this outing that I – or should I say, my class – was first told about the ghost. After spending most of the day at the theatre enjoying our exclusive tour, the guide relayed the story.

The class took their seats on the stage and, inside the dimly lit auditorium, the guide began to regale the ghost story of Robert Courtenedge; how he haunted the very theatre we stood in. In fact, the spot where he died was only a few yards from where we all sat, but we didn't know that... yet.

Robert was an employee of the theatre and, one evening, was at work tending to his duties. An opera on show at the time (*Nordisa*) was in full swing, and Robert decided to stop for a few minutes and watch the show from the side of the stage. During the show, a 36lb cannonball was rolled along a surface to create the sound of an avalanche. This was directly above where Robert was standing. After rolling its designated distance, the ball was supposed to have landed safely inside a wooden receptacle, but for an unknown reason, the ball ended up falling around 15ft on to the head of Courtenedge, caving in his delicate skull and killing him instantly. Ever since that dreadful incident, there has been an awful sense of melancholy in the theatre, and a strange ghostly presence.

His ghost is thought to meander around the stage area near to the spot where he died. Some say there is even a permanent shaft of ice-cold air, leading from the spot on the stage where he died to where the cannonball broke free on that tragic night. However, I have stood in the spot where Bob died and can recall no specific cold area. The likelihood is that any anomalous cold spot in that area will be discontinuous – meaning it will be reported every now and again as opposed to being permanent – if there really is cold spot anyway.

Robert is also thought to haunt a seat, high up in one of the balconies. He has been spotted sitting motionless in a chair by various members of staff. It is always the same chair he is seen in by all accounts, yet no one knows why he should want to haunt this particular seat. Perhaps the

Above *An artistic representation of Robert Courtenedge (or Bob), the ghost that is said to haunt the area to the side of the stage in the Tyneside Theatre. (Courtesy of Michael J. Hallowell, Thunderbird Craft and Media)*

Top *The Journal Tyne theatre on Westgate Road. Another well-known ghost haunts this venue. He is a former employee of the theatre, who died here in a horrific accident.*

answer is simply that the chair was randomly chosen by Bob to sit in and look down upon his treasured place of work, for it was believed that he dearly loved his job at the theatre. The last sightings of Bob occurred back in 2000, when, according to staff, he appeared on two Thursdays in a row during the pantomime season.

The ghost of a female, known as…wait for it…the Grey Lady, is also said to reside at the Journal Tyne Theatre, although the particulars of her ending, and why she pre-occupies the theatre, are somewhat unclear. Some say that her beloved ended their relationship, and so she hurled herself from the balcony to her death. Others say she fell by accident; know one knows for sure. Interesting that this tale bears a remarkable resemblance to the Theatre Royal ghost story, one thinks.

The Ghost of Jane (Jin) Jameson

The ghost of Jane Jameson is a very well-known account, but it is seldom told in the literature that deals with the area's folklore. I hope to amend things now, by bringing this old tale to the attention of the Tyneside folk once more. Before we delve into the story of this elusive phantom, however, we must first take a look at the woman herself, and how she fitted into the Tyneside area.

Jane, or Jin as she was known, was a young vagrant who was often seen around the city of Newcastle, more often than not in the Sandgate area, selling her wares. It was not just her 'wares' she sold to the local folk; she also became known as a 'woman of the night'.

By all accounts, she was a scruffy, half-dressed female who looked more like a man than a woman, and was rumoured to be 'hammered' all the time. She was also subject to unnecessary bursts of extreme violence. Jin was known to have had two illegitimate children, but they had both died in mysterious circumstances. People suspected, at the time, that Jin was responsible for their deaths, but nothing could be proved. The good folk of the Sandgate area were well aware of Jin, and her reputation, and stayed clear of her whenever they saw her. Eventually, she went to live in the Keelman's Hospital with her recently widowed mother, and the locals hoped, tentatively, that she might change her ways.

She lived at No. 5, which was on the ground floor of the building. After a while, at some point during 1828, she decided, without consulting her mother, to move in her lover, Billy Ellison. Now there were three people living in this small independent flat, which was really only fit for one person. On New Year's Day the following year (1829), Jin and her lover Billy had been on a drinking binge near the quayside. They had been downing ales and spirits for more or less the best part of the day, and were rather well-served to say the least. Once their money had run out, they returned to No. 5 and demanded more cash from Jin's poor mother.

Her mother, by this time, had endured as much as she was going to take from her daughter, and so refused to give her any more money for her alcoholic indulgences. An argument broke out between the two women and, as tempers flew, the mother accused Jin of killing her children. This provocation proved too much for Jin, who,

The Keelman's Hospital on City Road in Newcastle was the one-time home of Jin Jameson, one of Tyneside's most infamous scruffs; now one of Tyneside's most famous ghosts.

in a fit of rage, grabbed the red-hot poker from their burning fireplace and thrust it hard into her mother's chest. The heat melting the skin and her internal organs was something akin to putting a hot knife through soft, warm butter. Jin's mother stood no chance whatsoever and died a few days later from her injuries.

Jin, racked with remorse, explained to the authorities what had happened and was subsequently taken away and questioned. Her mother, before she died, had attempted to cover up the attack by claiming she fell on the poker by accident, but this pretence was not taken seriously and Jin was arrested for the killing.

Her trial began in March 1829, and because she could afford no defence council, she needed to come up with a plan to save her own skin. She ended up accusing her lover, Billy Ellison, of committing the murder, saying he had kicked her mother to death with his steel-capped boots. A host of witnesses testified against this notion; Jin was found guilty of murder and was sentenced to be hanged by the neck until dead on the town moor in Newcastle. A few weeks later, she was carted up to this location and strung up before a baying crowd of around 25,000 people. After hanging for just under twenty minutes, with her hands tied behind her back, she

Newcastle quayside, prior to the lavish law courts building that now stands on this spot. This is the area where Jin Jameson still resides to this day. (Courtesy of Walter Ritson)

The John Wesley memorial in Sandgate. This is the area of the quayside where Jin's ghost has been seen asking passers-by to bring her lover.

was cut down from the gallows and her body was taken away to be dissected by the barber surgeons. This was not the end of Jin though, not by a long shot. If the Tyneside folk thought they could get rid of Jane Jameson, they were wrong – for her ghost still walks.

One of Jin's favourite haunts is around the streets of Sandgate on the quayside, where she is known to appear to weary folk late at night to ask if they can help find her lover, Billy Ellison. She pleads with them to bring her lover, before disappearing as quickly as she appeared. It is hardly surprising that Billy's ghost has not been reported with her, presumably because he wants absolutely nothing to do with her.

Bessie Surtees House, Newcastle upon Tyne

Located on Newcastle's historic quayside is Bessie Surtees House. This is where the daughter of a wealthy merchant and former mayor of Newcastle once lived. She is said to have fallen in love with John Scott, the first Earl of Eldon. This relationship was frowned upon by Bessie's family and a strict ban was put on their liaisons. From a window in Bessie Surtees House, it is said that she climbed out and onto the back of a horse, which John Scott had waiting for her, and the two fled the scene to live life unhindered over the border in Scotland.

They galloped on horse back up Dog Leap Stairs, which is round the corner and at the foot of Dean Street. John and Bessie escaped, but their pursuers are said to have gotten only halfway up the steep flight of

stairs before tumbling back down, resulting in the deaths of a number of horses and their riders. It is the sound of the horses that supposedly haunts Dog Leap Stairs. There are, however, rumours that Bessie herself haunts the area as well. Witnesses have claimed to see her staring out of the very window she climbed through on the night of 18 November 1772.

The building is now in the hands of English Heritage and it is used as their North East offices. It stands five storeys high, with each level slightly overhang-

Bessie Surtees House in Newcastle; not just home to English Heritage, but also to a North East legend that dates back to the 1770s.

FROM THE ABOVE WINDOW
ON NOV 18ᵀᴴ 1772
BESSY SURTEES DESCENDED AND ELOPED WITH
JOHN SCOTT LATER CREATED 1ˢᵗ EARL OF ELDON
AND LORD CHANCELLOR OF ENGLAND

It is said that the young lady climbed out of this window and onto the back of a horse which her lover had waiting for her.

ing the one below it. It is a rare example of Jacobean architecture, with its interior being beautifully oak-panelled and luxuriant plaster ceilings hanging high over the old wood flooring. I remember, back in 2004, visiting the offices to attend a meeting with English Heritage. The team I was working with at that time were in negotiations with them regarding the potential investigations of a number of their wonderful properties. I remember walking through a passage as we headed off to the meeting room and, approaching the foot of the old wooden stairwell, I heard the sound of footfalls behind me. I turned around and there was no one there.

Upon querying this with the English Heritage staff, I was told that no one else was in the building – bar us – and that the sound of footfalls along that very passage was one of the most reported ghostly phenomena in the building.

Mrs Denton, Byker

Due to the nature of this story, and the time period it relates to, the names mentioned herein have been changed. The actual witness to the ghost sighting (my source for this story) has requested his own anonymity. As well as this, anonymity of the family concerned was asked for, due to the fact that certain family members are still alive. My source does not want to cause any undue distress to the relatives of the deceased. Bar this, the story you are about to read happened exactly as it is written.

The junction on Shields Road where it meets with Brinkburn Street, in Byker, was the scene of an unusual ghost sighting back in 1955, by a young apprentice cobbler whom we shall call Robert. This sighting occurred during daylight hours, when it was least expected. Furthermore, Robert didn't realise he had actually seen a ghost until a few days after the actual event, whereupon subsequent information came to light. Robert had been working at the local cobbler shop on Shields Road from early on that morning, and was on his way for some lunch at a nearby shop. As he was making his way down Shields Road, he happened to glance up to see an elderly lady making her way towards him, in amongst all the other midday Saturday shoppers. He recognised the woman as a friend of the family and so said hello to her as she meandered past him. Mrs Denton, for that was her name, said hello back and a short conversation ensued. After asking Robert how his family were, and then saying goodbye, she strolled on up Shields Road and out of sight. Robert, thinking nothing of this, carried on with his journey to get his lunch, and then returned to work and got on with his cobbler duties.

A few days went by and Robert was sitting at home around the tea-table with his family, eating their evening meal. Suddenly, Robert remembered his chat with Mrs Denton and so piped up that he had seen

The junction on Shields Road where it meets Brinkburn Street, in Byker, was the scene of an unusual ghost sighting in 1955.

her the Saturday previous. Then, he relayed her message to the family. A bemused look appeared on his mother's face, as she turned to Robert and said, 'Are you sure son…Saturday gone?' Robert confirmed it was the day that he had walked past her, and re-iterated the fact that she had asked him how the family was doing. Robert's mother turned to his father and muttered something quietly, to which he nodded his head. She then turned to Robert and solemnly said, 'Son, you couldn't have see Mrs Denton last Saturday because she died early last week.'

Robert gave this some considerable thought, and wondered just how he could have seen a woman in the flesh who had died a week earlier. Had he got his days mixed up? No, Robert knew the day was in fact Saturday, as this was the one day of the week he worked. The rest of the week he was at school, so he was 100 per cent sure of what day it was. Upon asking his family when Mrs Denton had passed over, he was told it was most certainly one week prior to his 'chat' with her. This left him dumbfounded, because the only possible answer left was that the young lad had seen the ghost of Mrs Denton, making her way up Shields Road that Saturday back in 1955.

One wonders why, and how, in fact, the woman was able to be seen, complete with shopping trolley, walking stick and handbag. Furthermore, if it was a ghost of the deceased woman, it is rather strange to think that Robert and Mrs Denton actually had a conversation during this brief, but ever so odd, encounter.

Many people suggest that sightings like this are 'stone tape' ghosts or 'psychic recordings', where events are somehow recorded, or transfixed, into the fabric of surrounding buildings or, indeed, the earth, and then – when the time or the conditions are right – they are played back to those lucky enough to see them. Had Mrs Denton, however, not spoken to Robert, we may presume a psychic recording could have accounted for the sighting, should this theory prove to hold validity of course. Having said that, had she not spoken that day to Robert, we may never have even found out about the apparition in the first place. The likelihood is that Robert would never have brought it up at the dinner table at all. It was only mentioned over dinner as Mrs Denton had enquired after the family.

I am fortunate enough to have been given permission to detail this fascinating case, and for this I am eternally grateful to my source. So, next time you are meandering up Shields Road doing your weekly shop, and you approach the junction of with Brinkburn Street, keep your eyes peeled and your ears to the ground because the little old lady who has just walked past you, complete with shopping trolley, walking stick and handbag, may well have been Mrs Denton, who died in 1955.

The Locomotive, Byker

Our next story takes place about three-quarters of a mile away, at the other end of the aforementioned Brinkburn Street, where it junctions with Walker Road in Byker. The pub, once called the Locomotive, stood opposite the British Engines Factory establishment, but has now, sadly, been long demolished. The pub was a fine old drinking establishment, which kept the Byker and Walker locals in ales and beers. I daresay those working at nearby British Engines and Hawthorn Leslie's – which is now the area known as St Peter's Basin – may have called in after work to whet their whistles before nipping home for a home-cooked evening dinner. I remember being inside the pub once, after calling in to use the loo during a bike ride with my father. I was only about ten years old, so sadly I couldn't sample the ales and beers that everyone else was so happily supping down.

Anyway, the ghost tale surrounding this pub came from the father of one of my old school friends, who often drank (the father that is) at the pub after spending his days hard at work along the road in Newcastle city centre. The tale is not so much associated with the pub itself but with the car park that stood outside. Albert, for that is what my friend's father was called, told me the tale when I was at my friend's house one night after school many, many years ago. He spoke of a strange figure dressed in old-fashioned clothing dating from around the 1940s. This character was often seen in the car park, skulking around and generally looking as though he was up to no good. We were told that many people coming to and from the pub had seen this strange-looking man, but, oddly, if they turned to take another look at him – they would find he was nowhere to be seen – he seemingly vanished into thin air in an instant. A harrowing aspect about this individual is that,

The Locomotive pub in Low Walker. Long demolished, the car park was the scene of several harrowing sightings. (Courtesy of Walter Ritson)

according to Albert, no one managed to ever get a look at his face. We were told that those who saw him were unable to recognise his facial features – as if they were blurred out! Now, to me a man that can disappear in an instant without a trace and without a face (rhyme not intended) – who is dressed in 1940s clothing, thirty years or so after that fashion had been around – can only be described as a spook, but whether or not this tale is genuine, I cannot really say for sure.

Most folk who drank in the pub have probably passed away by now. Even Albert is now sadly no longer with us, so I can't ask him any more about it. I have researched the area but cannot come up with any names, or records of any 'occurrences' dating back to the 1940s that could account for the strange phenomena. I wanted to corroborate the story and find an element of truth in it, but sadly this was not to be. That's not to say Albert was telling two daft school kids a tall story to try and scare them – although that thought has crossed my mind. The story may well have some truth in it; most tales like this usually do. Even if Albert was mistaken in a few details, or even 'hamming' up the tale to scare us, there is always an original source for such stories and it is these original sources that I am after. My only hope now is to sit back and wait, hoping that a former patron of the pub will get in contact with me. There must be someone! Perhaps they remember seeing this mysterious man for themselves or, indeed, remember the stories surrounding him. If there is such a person out there, reading these words right now, please do drop me a line; I would love to find out more.

The Ghost and the Tea Set, Byker

The following story is one of my favourite tales in this entire book. It comes from a very reliable source indeed: my father. I have relayed some of his other ghost sightings in previous books, including *Haunted Newcastle*, as he has had a few encounters over the years. This, I guess, is just one of my many reasons for being interested in ghosts, so, in a way, I have a lot to thank him for. The ghost tales he relayed to me as a child growing up have helped to shape my fascination, my passion, my love for the supernatural, and without this influence I may never have put pen to paper. Both of us have experienced many strange things, but as of yet my mother, Jean, and my brother, Gary, have not had any supernatural encounters. It does illustrate the point that not all people are susceptible to the paranormal. I guess my father and I simply are.

The tale centres on my father's childhood home on Carville Road in Byker. It dates back to the early 1950s, when he was thirteen years old. In his words:

I am writing this ghost account from memory, and to the best of my knowledge it is correct in all details. It started one night in 1952, when I was thirteen years old. My mother, Winifred, woke up screaming from a bad dream. She told me that in her dream, she was sitting up in her bed whilst at the same time looking across the room into her large dressing mirror. In the centre of the dressing table mirror was a small black dot and it was this what my mother was looking at [*sic*].

Carville Road in Byker (c. 1960). This was the area where my father grew up and where, in 1952, his grandmother (my great-grandmother) made her presence known to the family…after her death. (Courtesy of Walter Ritson)

An illustration of the woman in black that was seen in my grandmother's dream. (Courtesy of Michael J. Hallowell, Thunderbird Craft and Media)

The black dot suddenly began to get bigger and bigger. Eventually, the black dot in the mirror materialised into the form of a woman. Soon, details in the woman's face could clearly be seen. The woman was in a sitting position, was wearing a black dress and was said to have had 'sad eyes'. Her hands were held one over the other, resting firmly on her lap. It was at this point that my mother woke up, clearly distressed.

The next day my mother told her mother about the dream she had and described the woman who was wearing the black dress. My mother's mother calmly said to my mother that the woman in the dream was *her* mother. She said that she knew what this was all about and she was not to worry about it. She had 'come for her' by all accounts,

and [she said] 'it is soon to be my time'. Two days later my grandmother passed away. A week or so passed and the funeral came and went. During the clearing-out process of my grandmother's house, to sort out papers and other such documents etc., my mother picked up an old bunch of photographs and began to flick through them. In one of the pictures was the woman that had appeared in my mother's dream and was recognised immediately. Although her mother had already explained to her just who the woman in the dream was, she was rather surprised to have it confirmed this way, and so when she first ran her eyes over it, she jumped with a start, screamed, and dropped the pictures upon the floor. The photograph was placed to one side with all the other 'things to keep', but it was never seen again.

In the meantime, a tea set that had been promised to my sister ever since she was five years old was still at our house. My sister lived in Wales (and still does to this day) but never received her tea set due to an argument she had had with my mother. My mother point-blank refused to send it on to her, despite her mother's promise that she [my sister] could have it. A few months later, there was an organised tea party at our house and the special bone-china tea set was dug out and used. After the tea party was finished, the guests left our house and the tea set was left out on the table downstairs overnight; it was to be put away again at first light. In the middle of the night I was woken up to the sound of cups and saucers clinking and chinking, and the sounds of spoons rattling around as though the tea party

Back in 1952, a strange phenomenon occurred with an old tea set in my father's childhood home. (Courtesy of Michael J. Hallowell, Thunderbird Craft and Media)

had resumed. I thought that my father was up and about making himself a cup of tea and thought nothing more of it, until I got up for breakfast early the next morning. When I went downstairs I was greeted by a serious-looking mother and father and firmly asked, 'Just what the hell were you doing up in the middle of the night playing with the good china tea set?' I explained that I was not up at all through the night, but I too had heard the commotion but actually thought it was them. Apparently it had not been them either! With this, the tea set was immediately washed, packed up, and then posted to my sister in Wales – all within one hour.

An old photograph of my grandparents, Winifred and Walter Ritson (the central couple in the picture). It was Winifred that had a dream about the woman in black. (Courtesy of Walter Ritson)

I am in no doubt that it was my father's grandmother (my great-grandmother) that had come and tinkered with her old tea set, reminding her daughter, Winifred, that it should be in Wales with her granddaughter. The fact that my great-grandmother's wish was ignored, or disrespected, simply because of a personal grievance between my grandmother and her daughter, was enough, I think, to bring the spirit back from beyond to tie up these loose ends; a classic ghost tale of someone coming back from the dead to make something right.

The Roman Soldier, Walker

During my many years of investigating ghosts, I have heard a wealth of wonderful supernatural tales, many of them being truly chilling. It's incredible to think that these things do happen to normal, everyday people. Back in the late 1990s, I re-devised a questionnaire that I had originally drawn up in 1990, for individuals that had a strange tale to tell. Over a few years, I managed to collate between 300 and 400 completed forms. One day, I got chatting to the sales girl in the local camera shop on Shields Road. I was in there collecting my photographs of a recent trip to a haunted venue, when, of course, the subject of ghosts came up. We discussed the contents of my pictures and the sales girl, who was called Sharon, asked me about my visits to different haunted locations. She then expressed an interest in the topic of ghosts, simply because she herself had experienced a few strange occurrences over the years, with one in particular that had frightened her somewhat. She told me what had happened one night in 1994, and I was so convinced that she was telling the truth, I asked her if she would be prepared to fill in one of my questionnaires. The next week I popped into the shop to collect the form, and it is from this very questionnaire, which I still have filed away, that I relay the tale to you now.

The story is not a long-winded one, neither is it packed with over-exaggerated claims of blood-curdling terror. It began while Sharon was at her home near the Fosse public house in the Walker area of Tyneside, back in 1994. At 12.15 a.m. one morning, she decided to retire to bed, so she got up from her chair, cleaned her teeth and washed, before slipping on her nightgown and jumping into bed. As she was lying in her bed next to her husband, she suddenly heard the sound of footsteps creeping down the flight of stairs in her house. Her husband woke up in time to hear the tail-end of the footfalls. Sharon jumped out of bed and checked her childrens' rooms, as she thought it may have been one of them making their way downstairs. However, she found them both fast asleep in their beds; it was not them. She was quite perplexed as to who, or what, made this distinctive sound.

A few months passed and she thought nothing of it, until one night she heard the sounds again; only this time she knew she was in the house alone! Absolutely terrified, she slowly crept out of bed. As she peered down the stairwell, she could clearly hear movement at the bottom of the stairs, but no one was there. This really frightened her now, as now she knew there must be something inexplicable going on in her house. Again, morning came and went and before long, it was all forgotten.

A few months on and Sharon was in the house with her husband one night, when they both decided to head downstairs for a drink of water. They approached the top of the stairwell, put on the light and were both gobsmacked to see a Roman soldier at the foot of their stairs! The soldier, they said, stood motionless and facing the front door; he was also completely silent. They both stood there, watching this figure for about five minutes, glancing at one another once in a while. Not knowing what to do, the couple retreated back into their bedroom. The next time they glanced down the stairwell, the soldier was gone.

The first thing the couple did was check the front door. Had it been left open or unlocked? Perhaps someone dressed in Roman attire could have mistakenly entered the wrong house after becoming drunk at a fancy-dress party? An obscure and unlikely scenario, but it's just as obscure as seeing a real Roman soldier in your home in 1994, wouldn't you say? This notion was soon eliminated, however, after they tried their front door and found it was securely locked – as was their back door – and all their windows were closed too. This sighting remains a mystery to Sharon and her husband, as they know full well there was no one else in their house at that time. They concluded that it must have been the ghost of a Roman soldier in their home, but why and how were the questions on their lips.

Well, when I found out about this amazing tale, it struck me immediately that it must have something to do with the nearby A187 road, better known as the Foss Way, which runs behind Sharon's house.

The Foss Way road near Wallsend. It was not far from here that a sighting of a Roman soldier occurred in 1994.

A Foss (or Fosse) Way is a Roman-built road. The most famous of these was built from Exeter, in Devon, to Lincoln, in the East Midlands. Now, the Foss Way that runs behind Sharon's house heads east to west through Walker. Interestingly, it follows the route of Hadrian's Wall (built AD 122), which ran from Bowness-on-Solway to Wallsend. Had the Roman wall survived to this day in these parts of Tyneside, it would have stood directly behind Sharon's house. Sharon and her husband are one of many folk who happen to live on the site of the Roman wall, and quite possibly a Roman village or even a burial ground. This, I feel, could explain her sighting.

When I mentioned this to Sharon she went white; the penny had dropped. 'At least now I know we are not going mad,' she told me. Since that night in 1994, the Roman soldier has made no more appearances, indicating just how rare ghost sightings can be. Fear not though intrepid ghost hunter; if it's Roman ghosts you are looking for, then there are plenty to be found in Tyneside. At Newcastle Keep (*Pons Aelius*), a Roman sentry has been seen meandering around the foot of the castle on the site of the old Roman settlement. At Arbeia Roman Fort in South Shields, the phantom of a Roman has been seen patrolling the old fort silently at night. The Look Out pub in South Shields plays host to a centurion down in the cellar area, as does the Alum Ale House near the ferry landing. So, plenty of Romans roaming, if you pardon my pun.

Jonty's Ghost, Wallsend

During the course of my writing career, I have often relied upon one of my great pals to feed me ghost stories and strange tales of the supernatural. Mike Hallowell, as I have mentioned already in this book, is this friend, and by Jove does he know his stuff. I don't think there is a book on the shelves

Remains of the original Hadrian's Wall can be seen on the right, whereas the reconstructed wall, on the left, indicates just how thick and tall the wall once was.

with my name on it that Mike has not contributed to in some way. When I told him I was compiling a new book on Tyneside he asked, 'Do you have any tales of Wallsend for inclusion?' Unsure why he had asked this, I questioned him on the matter. 'Oh, its just that I have written up a cracking tale of ghostly goings-on from an old snooker hall, so I thought you may like this story,' he replied.

I never look a gift horse in the mouth, so I instantly said I would have it for the book, knowing that an exciting tale was sure to be in store. Instead of re-writing it entirely, however, as I usually do when I get drip-fed stories from the great man, I have decided – with Mike's kind permission of course – to reproduce his ghostly tale the way he told it, verbatim.

Even now, the name of Jonty Boomer is well-remembered in Wallsend. Before the Second World War, he ran a highly successful billiard hall in the town's Laburnum Avenue. Ah, but time moves on. Eventually Jonty went the way of all flesh, but he retained a place in the heart of the local community. Even after the billiard hall closed, the upper floor of the building, where the club operated from, was remembered as 'Jonty's place'. In the 1970s, the building was taken over by the Northern Card Company, who used it as a warehouse. Curiously, on the top floor, new owner Colin Walker found a collection of plastic footballs laid out in a triangle. They represented snooker balls, apparently, because this precise location used to be Jonty Boomer's favourite 'spot'. (Billiard and snooker players will no doubt grasp the metaphor.)

One day, in December 1974, Colin decided to move this strange, but nonetheless touching, epitaph to Jonty. This was a big mistake. Shortly after completing his tidy-up, a ludo board shot off a shelf and hit Colin on the back of the head. 'The board could not have fallen from the shelf, and there was no one else in the building at the time,' said Colin, who happened to be President of the Wallsend Rotary Club. 'It could only have been Jonty,' he added.

But Jonty, it seems, was responsible for many more ghostly goings-on in the warehouse. Lights would mysteriously switch themselves on and off, and the staff would hear weird footfalls on the top floor when no one was there. The manageress, Mrs June Parker, heard the eerie footsteps on numerous occasions when she was alone in the building, and admitted that the experiences made the hairs on the back of her neck stand on end. Despite the ghostly phenomena, no one felt that there was an 'evil presence' in the warehouse. They were all convinced it was simply Jonty. A medium, who was called in to investigate, even saw Jonty's disembodied face, but vouched that his presence was not malign in any way.

Mind you, this didn't mean that visitors to the establishment were never scared. On one occasion 'two burly joiners' called at the warehouse to affect some repairs. What they saw on the top floor isn't recorded, but afterwards they'd only work on the lower floors, where Jonty's spirit seemed less prevalent.

It's hard to be sceptical in cases like this, where there is so much eyewitness testimony. Staff, contractors and clients all saw

A billiard hall dating from around the same time as Jonty's haunted billiard hall, which once stood in Wallsend. (Courtesy of the Shields Gazette*)*

and heard things which have no rational explanation. Why did Jonty, albeit in disembodied form, throw the ludo board at Colin Walker? Apparitions are notorious for disliking changes made to the environment they haunt, and it is likely that the alterations made by the building's new owners irritated the phantom.

Still, the staff took the incident in good spirit, if you'll excuse the pun. Even the local press described Jonty's spirit as 'the friendly ghost of the High Street'. My feeling is that, had the upper floor been left alone – it was 'Jonty's place' remember – Colin would not have been so unceremoniously admonished. Perhaps giving Colin

a whack on the back of the head with a board game was Jonty's way of letting him know he wasn't too happy with some of the changes taking place. Locals don't talk about Jonty's ghost so much now. Perhaps he's finally started to enjoy his retirement in the spirit world – well-earned after running a busy billiard hall for all those years.

Willington Mill

At Willington Quay in North Tyneside – and less than a mile from my house – there once stood a flour mill. The factory was the first steam-driven mill in the North East and was owned by two cousins, George Unthank and Joseph Procter. Unthank and Procter were both devout members of the Society of Friends, or Quakers, and were renowned for their integrity and impeccable honesty. This, perhaps more than anything, made it harder to dismiss Procter's assertion that the mill house he lived in was well and truly haunted.

Two hundred years before the mill was built, a witch lived in an old cottage on the same site. Even then, the location was believed to be cursed. Whatever the truth, Joseph Procter didn't need much convincing.

A nursemaid once heard bizarre noises, described as heavy footsteps, coming from a room on the second floor of the mill house. At the same time, the window in the nursery below started to shake violently. On another occasion, footsteps were heard coming down the stairs, followed by the sound of the door to the house opening. Procter dashed out and found the door open – but nobody there.

It wasn't just the mill house that was haunted, though. The mill itself was infested by spectres, including the ghost of a woman known as 'Kitty', who was horribly injured in an accident there back in the early 1900s. By this time, the mill was no longer producing flour. It had been turned into a ropery, and Kitty had seemingly caught her hair in between two of the rollers. Kitty died within minutes and her shade has been said to haunt the mill ever since.

As well as ghosts, Willington Mill was also notorious for sightings of mystery animals, including a strange, cat-like creature with a long snout, a monkey that teased the children in the mill house, and an incongruous donkey-like creature that startled two engineers before disappearing. Over the years, numerous attempts were made to solve the mystery. In July 1840, chemist and South Shields councillor Tom Hudson stayed in the mill house overnight with a companion, Dr Edward Drury from Sunderland.

At first, the men – who were stationed on the landing of the upper floor – heard nothing, but shortly after midnight, they could hear what sounded like small feet pitter-pattering inside one of the rooms.

Hudson seemingly fell asleep – although he claimed he was actually 'resting his eyes' – and it was then that Drury caught sight of the ghost. According to the doctor, the grey-coloured spectre of an old woman floated from a closet within one of the rooms. Her right hand was clutched to her chest, as if she was in pain, and her left hand pointed towards the floor.

Drury watched in horror as the ghost slowly drifted towards Hudson and raised its hand, as if to place it upon his head. Drury – foolishly or bravely, make your own mind up – lunged at the ghost and ended up falling on top of the slumbering Hudson. The doctor's terrified shrieks woke Hudson up, but by that time the spirit had evaporated into the ether. It was later rumoured that both the doctor and the chemist had taken a brace of pistols with them, but had left them downstairs. This is only half the truth. In fact, it was Drury who had taken them both, but Hudson instructed him to leave them downstairs rather than upset their host, who, being a Quaker, was also a pacifist and disliked the use of firearms.

In 2009, Mike Hallowell and I carried out extensive research into the haunting of Willington Mill, and discovered things

Opposite, top *Willington Mill in North Tyneside, the scene of a remarkable haunting. One of the most famous ghost sightings in psychical-research history occurred in 1840. (Courtesy of Bridon Ropes)*

Opposite, bottom *A rare view of the Willington Mill complex (c. 1850). Note, the rear of the haunted house can be seen to the right of the lamp-post. (Courtesy of Bridon Ropes)*

that no one has ever come across before. This case, the haunting, is not at all how it appears. The day-to-day diary of events allegedly penned by Joseph Procter at the time of the hauntings (which are filed away in the Society for Paranormal Research (SPR) archives in Cambridge University), is also not what it seems. Murders, cover-ups, apparitions, poltergeist activity, mysterious hidden cellars and tunnels, mediumship and mayhem, have all been uncovered and published in the book detailing our research and our findings (*The Haunting of Willington Mill*).

The Chirton Silky

Ghost books, for me, are not just pages of spooky accounts that must prove the authenticity of these otherworldly denizens; on the contrary, if a ghost story is believed but has false or misinterpreted origins, then I feel it's my job, as a ghost investigator, to try to put the record straight. Most ghost tales I write about, I find to be true, and although the vast majority of people love to hear these 'true accounts' of the paranormal, there are some that love to hear them 'debunked' as well. I like to debunk ghost stories myself – good investigators should – but only if they are not true, of course. If I find truth in the tales, then I will say so; likewise, I will say so if I find untruths or

inconsistencies in the account. It would be easy to write a book about ghost tales that I have 'debunked', as opposed to penning works of ghost tales that are true. The following account is one of the ghost legends that I have found out to be just that – a legend.

For years, the area that was known as 'Silky's Lane' in Chirton, North Tyneside was reputed to be haunted by a ghost; a 'silky', as a matter of fact. Or is it fact? For I have came into possession of a photocopied, and sadly undated and unnamed, page of text from an old paper or magazine, which suggests there never was a ghost there in the first place. After doing a little digging around, I found that the article may date to around the 1920s, but I cannot be sure. It was penned by a local historian, William S. Garson, and it is entitled, 'The Origin of Our Local Ghosts'. Intrigued? I thought you might be.

Archibald Campbell, the tenth Earl and First Duke of Argyll, had been in exile in Holland with King Charles II, and according to my article, had also accompanied King William III (1650–1702) to England. He lived at Chirton Mansion for a long time during the aforementioned King's reign. Campbell was a great lover of horses and horse racing, and kept a large stud at his mansion. He also had fifty dogs – presumably hunting dogs – and around sixty sheep. His rebellious and extravagant behaviour was well known around the Chirton, North Shields area, and if there was ever any scandal or gossip, you could bet your bottom dollar that Archibald Campbell would be in the thick of it. However, he was often told by the lady of the house, one Mrs Allison (not his wife), that his wildman antics would be the 'death of him', and sure enough she was right.

In September 1703, he received 'many bruises in a night revel in a house situated on the bank side near the foot of Stephenson Street, and subsequently died a few days later.' One presumes his unruly and scandalous antics got him into trouble while attending a party, which subsequently led to a fracas. We presume this fracas was his last, and it is thought he must have been beaten to death. After his death, his body was prepared for its journey back to Argyll in Scotland, and it was taken back by horse and carriage. His belongings were returned by sea, but the boat carrying his prized possessions, worth thousands of pounds (millions of pounds in today's money), sank on its journey and never made it back to Scotland.

Mrs Allison, now the proud owner of Chirton Mansion, decided to sell the house and was paid the handsome sum of £1,200. With this she set up home nearby, but within months of her new-found fortune and fame, she too was dead. As you can imagine, the local gossip spread like wildfire about just how Mrs Allison had died. Of course, they came to the conclusion that she was murdered for her money, as 'there would have been no chance of a natural death, not so soon after inheriting such a fortune.' No, it was decided that there must have been foul play involved, and because the locals decided her 'murder' must have been a gruesome one too, it was obvious she would come back and haunt the area as a ghost. And there, my dear readers, is how the ghost of Chirton came to be.

It appears that through the idle gossip and chit-chat of local folk, all unfounded and with no evidence to back up their stories whatsoever, the ghost of Chirton was born. Like all ghost stories, after a while it became rooted in the area's history and, through the passage of time, it took hold and eventually passed down to future generations, who in turn passed on their own version of the story. I wonder how many more ghost stories we know that have begun this way?

The Black Dog of Shields

The 'Black Dog' phenomenon dates back hundreds of years, with the first actual sightings probably being around the early 1100s. These 'Hell Hounds', or 'Devil Dogs', were once believed to be harbingers of death, and in some cultures they still are, but many reports suggest otherwise. People have stated that these apparitional hounds have appeared from out of nowhere, pacing alongside them until a looming danger (one unknown to the witness until after the dog mysteriously disappears) has passed, as though they have been assigned – for those few moments in time – to act as a guardian or protector. Perhaps there are different types of apparitional dogs, some bad and some good; some that protect and guard, and others that are harbingers of doom. The evidence suggests this could be the case.

Normally reported at dusk or during night time, and usually in old country lanes, dark roads and cemeteries, these 'Black Dog' apparitions have been seen in all sorts of shapes and sizes. However, there are a number of distinguishable features that all witnesses notice. They all comment on their large, glowing-red eyes, and their razor sharp teeth that drool with stinking saliva as they stand and stare intently at you.

The 'Black Dog' sightings have, for the most part, been observed in England. Wherever you may decide to roam, whether it is in the North of England or in the West Country, you are not safe from this phenomenon. Of course, wherever you are, you will find that the names of these spectral hounds differ; same phenomenon, different name. In Norfolk they are known locally as 'Black Shuck' or 'Old Shuck'. In Staffordshire the 'Black Dog' ghost is known as 'Padfoot'. In Yorkshire it is known as 'The Barguest', and in Lancashire as 'Skriker'. Up here in the North East of England (yes, I am afraid we are not exempt from this phantom animal), it is known simply as 'Shuck' or 'Shock'.

Meandering through the pages of, what I consider to be, the best volume in existence on mysterious animals and cryptozoological fauna, I came across a terrifying story of our very own 'Black Shuck'. There are, however, other accounts of 'Black Dog' sightings in the region (mainly Northumbria), but not many. Detailed in Michael J. Hallowell's magnificent tome *Mystery Animals of Northumberland and Tyneside*, is the story of the 'Black Dog of Shields' – simply 'shields' because, as you will read, no one is sure if the ghost-dog haunts South Shields or North Shields. You see, there are two versions of the narrative, with

An artistic representation of the 'Black Dog' of Shields. This ghost-hound is thought to haunt the old yards around North Shields quayside, although some would argue it's a South Tyneside spectre. (Courtesy of Michael J. Hallowell, Thunderbird Craft and Media)

only the location in the account differing. Since they are both in Tyneside, they sit well within these pages.

The legend comprises of one horrific death and two different phenomena, all combined into one chilling narrative. In the early 1830s, North Shields and South Shields were, like nowadays, inhabited by both decent folk and undesirables. Burglary was commonplace, and not many people would venture outside after dark. A family living in the borough at that time consisted of three members: a husband and his wife, and their grown-up son (nicknamed Fatty), who was often away at sea. One night, after a sea trip had ended early, he arrived back to the area. Not wanting to stay on board his vessel until morning, he made his way through the dark streets, until he reached his house in North Shields (or South Shields, depending on which story you believe).

He put his key in the door and crept inside, hoping not to disturb his parents, who were obviously fast asleep at such a late hour. He figured it would be a nice surprise for them to get up the following morning and find their beloved son safe and sound at home. Alas, this was not to be. During his fumbling around in the dark, he knocked over an ornament and his slumbering parents were alerted. He, perhaps, should have put on the light after making the din, but he decided not to. Big mistake; for his parents were sneaking down the stairs, getting ready to jump this intruder.

At the foot of the stairs, his father was confronted by a large, black silhouette and, believing it was a burglar, proceeded to beat him relentlessly. The man dropped to the floor unconscious, but the attack did not stop there. By now his wife had joined in the beating, which continued for a few minutes. Once they had finished issuing the 'good hiding', they turned on the lights. There, lying in a pool of blood, was the lifeless corpse of their beloved son. You cannot begin to imagine their horror when they realised the tragic misunderstanding that had occurred.

It appears no charges were brought against Fatty's parents, as it was agreed by the jury that this was nothing more than a tragedy. This, however, was not the end of Fatty. His ghost was allegedly seen inside the house by his parents and, on a number of these occasions, he was accompanied by a spectral black dog! After a while, Fatty ceased to haunt the house altogether, but the mysterious animal continued to be spotted. Many stories have circulated as to where the dog actually came from. Some say it was a childhood pet of Fatty's; others say the dog was starved to death in the hold of Fatty's ship, after he had befriended and smuggled it into England. No one knows for sure.

Reports continued to come in of the spectral hound and, worryingly, they took on the sinister description of the more conventional 'Black Dog' or 'Shuck', with large red eyes and protruding teeth. Those who believe the story occurred in North Tyneside are still convinced, to this day, that 'Black Shuck' haunts the docks at North Shields. Those on the other side of the water believe the dog haunts the area where Fatty was believed to have lived, Melbourne Place. Fatty returned home on 31 October and met his grizzly end. It is said that on this date 'Black Shuck' returns from the dead to walk in Shields – but which one?

So, if by chance one day you stumble across a horrifying black dog, with glowing red eyes and razor-sharp fangs, and it happens to be 31 October, do give me a call and let me know which 'Shields' you are in – North or South. Oh…and try to get a picture of it!

The Chain Locker, North Shields

The Chain Locker public house, near to the ferry landing in the old fishing village of North Shields, is sadly no longer a public house. Now converted into flats and offices, this one-time drinking den served regular commuters from both South and North Shields and acted as a great 'in-between' pub for revellers that were on their way into North Shields, and of course those that were on their way out to South Shields. Indeed, I frequented this pub myself on many occasions whilst waiting for the ferry to take me to South Tyneside on one of my nights out as a younger man. Prior to the pub becoming the Chain Locker in 1986, it was named the Crane House. It's such a shame that the old building is a tavern no more, as it was indeed a fine drinking establishment which boasted character, charm, and, allegedly, a ghost.

On one of my visits to the pub, while awaiting my friends, I got chatting to the then landlord and, of course, the subject of ghosts came up. I happened to ask if the pub had any resident spirits – not including the Whiskeys and the like up on the top shelf – and was surprised to hear that a strange encounter was 'had' in the premises some years earlier. 10.30 p.m. had came along and the dreaded 'last orders' at the bar had been called. The then bar manager had emptied out the pub of its clientèle, locked the doors, and was busy empting the ashtrays and collecting the glasses and bottles that had been left over from the night. Suddenly, the unmistakable sounds of footfalls were heard to clump across the wooden floor that he was standing on.

The Chain Locker pub (with the old Crane House sign still on the side of the building); the scene of an isolated, but very strange, paranormal incident many years ago.

He looked around and could see no one present, yet the footfalls continued right past him. Along with the strange footfalls, the bar manager also heard a whistling sound. Each note contained a vibrato leading me to think that the ghost – if ghost it was – was likely to be that of an elderly man. Those that have heard old men whistling out a tune will surely know what I mean.

I asked if they ever got to the bottom of what happened and was told they had not. The bar manager that had experienced this strange encounter was, by all accounts, 'a no nonsense, well educated young man', and 'would take all ghost stories with a huge pinch of salt', so hearing of the story from this very chap surprised everyone, as you could imagine. Explanations were sought but as I was told during my chat, 'the chap heard what he heard and was completely perplexed by it'. The ghost's identity was never established, neither has there been any more strange encounters in the bar; this was an isolated incident.

The Wooden Doll, North Shields

Situated at the top of a steep embankment close to Dockwray Square, just off Hudson Street in North Shields, the Wooden Doll public house commands spectacular views of the River Tyne Estuary. It is a comparatively old, traditional style boozer overlooking the famous North Shields Fish Quay and houses a wonderful beer garden from which the aforementioned views can be had. Over a pint of bitter, on a sunny day, one can view the magnificent ruin that is Tynemouth Priory and Castle behind the statue of Lord Collingwood. Looking south you can see across the Tyne, where the dramatic cliff tops of South Shields lie, and of course the wonderful town of South Shields itself. Both sides of the river offer amazing views, making the entire view a panoramic of sheer aesthetic beauty.

The pub is a quaint old building and oozes a certain charm. When you venture inside it is like taking a step back in time. With beautiful wooden flooring and old beams stretching across its low ceilings,

you certainly get that old-world feel. I have sat in this pub many a time supping a pint of real ale. On one occasion I paid a visit to the gents' during an afternoon session, after I had enquired as to where they actually were. This was one of my first visits to the inn and I was subsequently informed by the barman: 'Through the double doors and down the stairwell at the bottom of the building.' Now, as I ventured to pay my visit, I got a horrible feeling that there was someone with me. I knew there was not, as I looked around straight away and found I was the only person inside the stairwell. I felt as though my every step was being watched by someone, or something; I felt really uneasy.

Suddenly, I felt a chill and shuddered for a moment. I hurried into the lav, and then and hastily made my way back upstairs to my welcoming beer. As I walked back into the bar I had the urge to ask the barman if the pub was reputed to be haunted. The barman turned to me and said, 'Have you seen her then?' 'No,' I said, 'but I think I most definitely sensed something down there.' I was then informed by the barman that a paranormal investigation was once held at the pub by a respected team who had brought a medium to assist in their investigations. The same feelings that I had sensed on those stairs were exactly the same feelings that other people had sensed on the investigation. The visiting medium said the spirit was that of a woman and resided on that very stairwell.

So, is the Wooden Doll pub haunted? To date, I haven't heard of any other accounts, but that's not to say nothing has occurred. It would also be nice to put a name to the ghostly lady on the stairs – if, indeed, she

The Wooden Doll pub in North Shields.

does walk the stairwell of the Wooden Doll. That would mean organising another over-night investigation there, which, I am afraid, is not welcomed (at the time of my visit) by the new management.

The Nile Street Spectre, North Shields

On an unassuming street in North Shields town centre, the spectre of a 'grey, ghostly figure' is said to reside; that's according to a news clipping from *The Journal* dated 16 December 1974. It appears that one of the business properties down that way, Kemkleen Ltd, was said to be haunted, but the sceptical proprietor of that location, Fred Gallagher, was having none of it. He was, by all accounts, a big, burly man who was over 6ft in height and afraid of nothing.

For years it was said that no woman would venture into the building alone at night because of the strange, unexplained noises that often reverberated throughout it. Fred often mocked and scorned these women for believing the ghost was real, until one day, he and a fellow workmate saw it for themselves. Fred was thirty-five years old when he suddenly 'changed his tune' one night in the early 1970s, after admitting to seeing the ghost through a glass-panelled door inside the property. He said they could both clearly see 'the shape of a man's head and shoulders through the glass door', when they knew no one else was inside the building with them.

Fred told the newspaper reporter that they saw the figure as it moved away from the door and disappeared out of sight. Upon carrying out a thorough search of the premises, they found no intruder. All

Nile Street in North Shields town centre. It was here that a ghostly figure was seen to drift across the road early one morning.

these encounters back in the early 1970s? It would be fascinating to find out.

The Tynemouth Lodge Hotel

One of North Tyneside's most famous haunted pubs, the Tynemouth Lodge Hotel, sits alone on Tynemouth Road, not far from the village of Tynemouth itself. It has been a public house since 1799. Many years ago, a Working House of Correction stood close by and held criminals and law-breakers such as robbers, thieves and, more often than not, 'ladies of the night'. It is thought that well-to-do personages, such as law men and judges, would often lodge at the inn when they were in Tyneside on their law enforcement duties.

I have visited the Tynemouth Lodge Hotel on countless occasions, on my memorable pub crawls that have begun in the old fishing town of North Shields and finished in Whitley Bay seaside resort. I have always enjoyed this particular stop-off and found it to be a welcome retreat, where fine ales and beers keep you going until you reach the pubs and drinking dens down the coast.

One of my last visits to Tynemouth Lodge Hotel was a few years ago now. Although I did have a pint or two, this was not a visit to drink the alehouse dry, but instead to find out more about their resident ghost – or should I say their resident ghosts – as there is not one, but three! I was told that in the upper section of the pub and in the private living quarters, the ghosts of two Georgian children have been witnessed running happily between one of the rooms and the passageway. These two

the exits (which were downstairs) were locked behind them, and the passageway taken by the figure led to no exits at all, and they found no one when they followed it down there. With Fred was a chap named James Culham, who also vouched for the sighting of the ghost. He said, 'I am not the sort of person who sees things, but if there are such creatures as ghosts then this was definitely one.'

Outside, on Nile Street itself, the spectre of a grey figure was spotted early one morning by a paperboy as he was doing his round. He saw the figure emerge from the Kemkleen property and slowly drift across the street. Thinking this was something 'otherworldly', the young lad bravely approached the figure, whereupon it disappeared into thin air – right in front of his eyes. The two sightings have been linked, and are assumed to be one and the same spectre. Has the ghost been seen again since

children are closely followed by an older female figure, also dressed in Georgian attire, including an old bonnet. The whole scene is acted out silently, before it peters out into thin air in front of the bewildered onlookers. Maybe it is an older sibling who is chasing the youngsters? Or is it perhaps their mother or an aunt? No one knows for certain. What we do know is that the haunting seems, most certainly, to be a happy one, as smiles are abundant and excitement is shown upon their spectral faces. Perhaps if sound accompanied the apparitions, one would hear the thumping of feet upon the floor and the roars of laughter that often come with happy family scenarios just like this one. Rest assured, there is no chilly atmosphere in this pub, no feeling of being watched, and certainly no sense of untoward presences.

It is a most delightful haunting to say the least. In fact, this is one of the happiest hauntings I have ever had the pleasure of coming across

The Tynemouth Lodge Hotel, where three ghosts have been witnessed together on the upper floors of the building.

Tynemouth Priory

Owned by English Heritage, and undoubtedly one of Tyneside's most romantic and picturesque ruins, Tynemouth Castle and Priory really is a sight to behold. Standing gracefully on a diminutive outcrop overlooking the North Sea and the River Tyne Estuary, this one-time seventh century monastery is said to be the burial place of the former King of Northumbria, Oswin. In around 1090, the monastery was laid siege to by the Vikings; they took what they wanted and destroyed the rest, leaving this one-time great edifice in a ruinous state. After this, the land was acquired by Benedictine Monks and, subsequently, a priory was built on the site. This castle and priory were, at one time, the most well-defended in the entire region, playing a very important role during the border wars between the English and the Scots. Around the mid-1500s, the land was surrendered to King Henry VIII and the remaining monks at the priory were removed. Legend has it that one of these unfortunate monks still remains there to this day. He can be seen in

The ruins of Tynemouth Priory, standing desolate on the cliff tops. Legend has it that a monk haunts the area. He has been seen peering out to sea from the headland on cold, foggy mornings.

the atmospheric ruins, peering out to sea from the headland on cold, foggy mornings. No one knows for sure why he haunts the headland here. Perhaps he loved the priory so much that he simply wanted to stay there after his death. Perhaps his passing was a tragic and painful one at the hands of the Vikings, leaving his earthbound soul to roam the scene of his death? Having said that, his ghost has not been seen for a very long time now, so perhaps he no longer haunts the area; maybe he has found peace in his afterlife? Regardless of what has happened to the spectral monk of Tynemouth, his ghostly legacy lives on after all these years. Perhaps on one misty morning, his hooded form will be seen standing silently looking out to sea once more.

During one of my many visits to the priory, I decided to carry out an experiment of my own. I thought I would give the practice known as 'pendulum dowsing' a try, to see what (if anything) would happen. During my years of investigating the paranormal, I have seen with my own eyes some of the amazing results that dowsing can throw up; however, I always remain sceptical about the method of spirit communication itself, the information received, and the actual source of it. With dowsing, I am on the fence. I didn't have a suitable pendulum with me that day, so I used a gold ring suspended from a necklace. Makeshift pendulums can work just as well as real ones, so I thought to myself, why not? I steadied myself, held my makeshift communication tool up in front of me, and began my experiment.

Suddenly, it was set in motion and began to move slowly from left to right. Being in a ruined building, and on the blustery North East coast, I put this movement down to slight winds and draughts. However, what was to happen next left me flabbergasted. Suddenly, as I was standing there, not expecting anything remotely odd to occur, the pendulum was wrenched from my hands – with some force I might add – and flew threw the air. It continued to 'fly' through the air until it landed at the feet of a friend of mine called Suzanne. She was exploring the other ante-rooms of the gatehouse and just happened to walk into the area where I was. Her face was a picture and, by all accounts, so was mine! Was the wind responsible for this? I would have to say no, simply because I felt the thing being pulled from me. It was as though an invisible hand grabbed the ring and tugged it from me. With this, I decided to ask the staff about the ghosts. I was very much intrigued by what had just happened and was most interested to see if anyone else may have reported anything at the ruin. I was informed about their resident ghost, who is seen on foggy mornings on the summit of the headland, but, of course, we already knew about this ghostly monk. When I enquired if, per chance, there were any more, we were surprised to hear that a group of monks were apparently seen by a number of visitors in the priory grounds. This sighting took place a few years ago now, and occurred near the tall, ruined tower at the end of the priory, which is right next to the chapel. They were seen in a group, kneeling down next to the graves.

My final tale comes from, and concerns, my good friend Colin Nunn. Colin lives in California now, after emigrating there with his wife Cindy. He has given me permission to reproduce his story, and his pictures. Colin claims to have photographed a ghost, or at least an anomalous mist, while on a visit to Tynemouth Priory many years ago. The visit took place before I even became acquainted with Colin and his wife. The resulting photographs are, ultimately, what gave Colin and Cindy the 'push' to begin investigating strange claims of the paranormal. This is their story, in Colin's words:

I took these frames at Tynemouth Priory. I wanted to get a nice, clear shot of the stone figures within. While it was a nice, clear and bright day, the light within the chamber was limited; therefore in order to ensure I had a good clear exposure I had to mess around with various settings on the camera; exposure, flash, aperture etc., and take several frames, hoping at least one would be good. It was later, upon reviewing, that I noticed the mist I had captured throughout the frames, which appeared in different places, vanished, and then reappeared again in several places. The only conclusion I could make was that this mist, which was not visible with the naked eye, was moving around inside the chamber. I was not smoking at the time and there was no one else in the vicinity smoking. It was a perfectly clear day with absolutely no mist or fog. My lens had recently been cleaned using a professional and expensive kit. I have no explanation for the mist or its apparent movement and can only conclude it to be paranormal

The 'anomalous mist' observed at Tynemouth Priory. The photographer claimed that there was no actual mist at the time, and no one in the area was smoking. (Courtesy of Colin Nunn)

Here we can see the mist has depleted somewhat, but it is still vaguely visible. (Courtesy of Colin Nunn)

in nature. The camera used was a Fujitsu S620zoom, 3megapixel SLR.

Tynemouth Train Station

Tynemouth Metro is a former North Eastern railway station, which was opened in 1882. It once served the good folk of Tyneside between Newcastle and Whitley Bay, and is now a Grade II listed building. Eventually the line ceased operations for a while, until it was utilised once more when work began on the Tyneside metro system. This old line was then incorporated into the new network of metro lines that were snaking their way around the region, making it the oldest metro station in Tyneside. The same happened in other places in Tyneside too, with certain other old lines becoming re-used and brought back to life for a second incarnation. Of course, many new tracks were laid and new stations made during the construction of the metro system, which has resulted in the birth of 'Nexus'. Second only to the London Underground, this network of railways is most certainly one of the best ways to get around in our region. In 2007, the BBC News reported that English Heritage had issued a statement saying that Tynemouth Station was in dire need of restoration. Sadly, at the time of writing, the work is yet to be carried out on the station; only one small mid-section of the building has been refurbished so far. Well, it's a start!

My friend Mike Hallowell informs me that in 2004, several traders at the weekly indoor flea market, which is held on the platforms every Saturday and Sunday, claimed they saw the ghost of a woman in Edwardian attire. The female was reported to float around the stalls, as if she was actually looking for something. One woman said that this enchanting, extremely well-dressed lady even picked things up from her stall and looked at them, but when the stall holder tried to talk to the lady, she disappeared into thin air. Not much else is known about the ghost lady from Edwardian England, except the fact that this was – to the author's knowledge – the only time she has been seen here.

Phantoms on South Parade, Whitley Bay

Shopkeeper William MacFarlane got more that he bargained for when he moved his store into premises on South Parade, Whitley Bay. Little did he know at the time, but he was moving into a property that was already 'inhabited', albeit by an individual who was, shall we say, not of this world. It's ironic that South Parade, nowadays, is the place to be for weekend revellers and party goers, as the main drinking spots are located here. Bars and clubs line South Parade on both sides of the street, and they are stocked to the gills with all kinds of ales and spirits; of course, the spirits differ somewhat these days to those that haunted the old carpet shop many years ago. Not much is actually known about William MacFarlane, or the ghost that resided in his shop, but thanks to a faded old newspaper clipping (again, unfortunately, undated and unnamed), we know a little; and a little is more than enough to begin with.

South Parade in Whitley Bay.

The clipping I have is also, unfortunately, cut in half (that is the way it was given to me); therefore only half the story is told, as the lower half of the clipping is missing. Still, I feel this tale of ghostly goings-on should still be included herein, simply because it did occur, and the likelihood is that not many people will have heard about it. You never know, someone may read this story and shed some light on it; so, if anyone can fill in some of the missing gaps in regards to this creepy story, I would love to hear from you.

The words '…in his last shop, in South Parade', makes it clear that William MacFarlane moved from his premises in South Parade after experiencing the strange occurrences at the haunted location. Indeed, the article I gleaned this informa-

tion from was not published until after his move, indicating that he may not have been too happy to discuss his experiences during his time at the haunted shop. Curious incidences, such as doors flying open with no human intervention, occurred quite a lot by all accounts, causing staff considerable alarm, as you would expect. A gas fire that was kept in the building was also interfered with by the spook, much to the irritation of the staff, as this occurred usually on really cold days. The most impressive account comes from one of William's staff members; a cleaner, who reported seeing the 'spectre of an old coachman dressed in a tri-corn hat and knee breeches'.

William states in the short interview that he would often ask for lights to be turned on and off by the ghost, and it would often oblige him. On one occasion, when he asked for another demonstration of 'ghostly behaviour', he was rewarded with six rolls of felt being pushed over, crashing loudly to the floor. He states that these rolls were extremely heavy, and would have taken a very strong man to have pushed even one of them over. The frustrating thing about this old article is that the very last decipherable line reads, 'That building was exor...' – and that is where it cuts off. This, without doubt, was about to say that the building in question was exorcised in an effort to rid the premises of the ghosts, but we don't know what actually happened. What was the outcome? Who did the ceremony? And did it work? Well, I think I may be able to suggest an outcome. The likelihood is that the exorcism, or a blessing of the premises, was in actual fact carried out by the local priest, as is usually the case. The fact that William still moved out of the premises and into a new one, may indicate that he was fleeing the disruptive spirits. Therefore, in my final analysis, I suggest that the ritual exorcism carried out here had very little, if indeed any, effect whatsoever; but I may be wrong.

Curry's Point, Whitley Bay

Located at the end of a long, windy road, and near St Mary's Nature Reserve at Whitley Bay, is an area of headland known as Curry's Point. It was here – next to the car park – where convicted murderer Michael Curry swung in a gibbet cage, after committing murder most foul. A boulder marks the spot where this gibbet post once stood, with a commemorative plaque, placed there in 1989 to coincide with the 250th anniversary of this gruesome event. Upon it, the text explains what actually happened:

> On the 4th of September 1739 Michael Curry was executed for the murder of the landlord of the Three Horseshoes Inn at Hartley. His body was afterwards hung in chains from a gibbet at this spot within the sight of the scene of his crime. Ever since that dreadful event this headland has been known as Curry's Point.

Over the years, there have been reports of strange happenings in this area; indeed, some folk suggest it may be haunted. I heard some of these tales myself during a late-night radio phone-in show, many years ago now.

A young couple out for a drive one night, decided to pull into the car park for a bit of impromptu lovemaking. As they pulled in to their car-parking space, they saw in their headlights a tall, dark figure of a man. This man was motionless and seemed to be glaring straight into the car at the bewildered couple. Being somewhat unnerved, they turned out their headlamps, but decided to immediately turn them back on – just to see if he was still there. Within a split second of turning the lights off and then back on, this figure had somehow disappeared into the night, leaving the couple in no doubt that they had seen a ghost. Apparently, there was no way someone could have disappeared that quickly from view, either to the left or to the right, without being seen. Of course, I suppose there is a small possibility that it could have been someone out at night, trying to 'freak out' the couple in

Curry's Point headland in Whitley Bay, where the body of Michael Curry was gibbeted for killing a local landlord. The plaque was erected in 1989 to commemorate the 250th anniversary of the murder.

less gale-force winds from the North Sea pummel the land, and where the moon shines brightly down upon the lonely lighthouse and its rocky shores – really is the ideal setting for a ghost. With ingredients such as a gruesome murder, and an execution followed by a gibbeting, one would almost expect this place to be haunted. One thing is for sure; when the couple saw the figure in their headlamps, they decided not to stay and carry out their nocturnal activities. Perhaps next time it would be best for them to book into a room, making certain first, of course, that the hotel is not haunted too!

Seaton Deleval Hall

Standing majestically in Seaton Deleval, and facing the Cheviot Hills in the county of Northumberland, is the beautiful Seaton Deleval Hall. This really is one of Tyneside's most magnificent buildings, and has had the reputation for being haunted for many, many years now. In 1718, it was decided by Admiral Deleval that the old house, which he had just acquired, needed a complete renovation. Organisation of the work began, and in 1720 it was rebuilt by architect Sir John Vanbrugh. The building work took eight years to complete, but, sadly, Admiral Deleval never saw his finished home, for he died in a tragic accident one day after being thrown from his horse. His nephew and heir, Sir Francis Blake-Deleval, took the reigns, so to speak, and finished off what Admiral Deleval had started. In those days, it was common for families of this stature to have a 'seer', or a prophet, live with them. Their primary function

the car. Perhaps the 'ghost' was a night-time car thief in search of a joy ride? It could have been someone out walking their dog, who just happened to be caught up in the headlamps of the car. Who knows, perhaps the night walker was just as shocked and frightened as the couple? Or, could it have perhaps have been the ghost of Michael Curry, stalking the headland, haunting the area where his body was once hanged in chains and left to decay for all to see? There may be a rational explanation for this sighting, but you never know, do you?

When ones thinks about it, this small area of Tyneside – a dark headland, where in the dead of night the howling and relent-

was to see into the future and guide the family with key decisions, to improve their quality of life. The Delavals were no different, with a 'seer' in residence at the hall. They, of course, would have probably been better off without theirs, as he is said to have forewarned them that the next generation would bring no heirs to carry on their family name – not good news. Sir Francis Blake-Deleval had eight sons and five daughters, and by the time of his death, in 1771, they were all dead. It seems that the 'family seer' saw this. His brother, Sir John Blake-Deleval, then stepped into the breach and became the first Lord Deleval, until he passed away in 1808. The remaining family members (another John, his son, and Edward, his younger brother) died not long after, and the hall then passed to a family from Melton Constable in Norfolk, called the Astleys. This family was represented by the Marquis of Hastings.

Since the early 1800s, Seaton Deleval Hall has been the seat of the Hastings family and, like the Delavals, they had no luck with the house either. On 3 January 1882, a raging inferno tore through the hall and caused considerable damage to the

Seaton Deleval Hall is famously haunted by a ghost known as the White Lady. She is seen looking out of the windows of the great house. (Picture courtesy of Mark Winter)

property. The house was abandoned and for the next century, it lay derelict and uninhabitable. The hall remained empty until the 1980s, although there were attempts to restore and rebuild the hall in the 1860s and 1950s. During the 1980s, the west wing, which had been restored, was available and fit for habitation, so one Edward Henry Deleval Astley moved in until his death in 2007.

Seaton Deleval Hall is now looked upon by many as Sir John Vanbrugh's finest work, and one of Northumberland's greatest, most romantic houses. It is also considered to be one of the most important historic houses in Britain. Charles G. Harper said in his book *Haunted Houses* (1907), 'Monumental is Seaton Deleval, and full of eerie thrills for the visitor.' And indeed it is; the 'eerie thrills' are in abundance, due to the nature of the phantom that is said to reside there. She is known simply as the White Lady, and she has allegedly been observed standing in one of the windows, looking out. An acquaintance of mine, who went to school close by many years ago, told me that she often visited the hall during lunch breaks with her friends, to do a spot of ghost hunting of their own. 'It was always known to be haunted,' she said, and went on to explain: 'The ghost that haunted the hall was of Lady De La Val, who was thought to have been waiting for her long-lost love who went to war and, tragically, never returned.'

In the early 1990s, an alleged sighting of the White Lady was reported by a group of night-time adventurers, who visited the site after the hours of darkness. The hall was closed to the public at that time, of course, and the drive gates were locked, so they had to make do with investigating the building from the perimeter wall. Apparently, they all saw what looked like a white or greyish figure of a woman, looking from out of one of the windows. They said she turned around slowly and stepped back from the window before vanishing from sight. The hall, it seems, was completely empty. Whatever they saw certainly left its mark upon them.

Bibliography and Recommended Reading

Belanger, Jeff, *Encyclopaedia of Haunted Places: Ghostly Locales from Around the World* (New Page Books, 2005)

Harper, Charles G., *Haunted Houses* (Senate, 1907)

Harries, John, *The Ghost Hunters Road Book* (Letts, 1968)

Matthews, Rupert, *Mysterious Northumberland* (Breedon Books, 2009)

Price, Harry, *Poltergeist over England* (Country Life, 1945)

Ritson, Darren W., *Ghost Hunter: True Life Encounters from the North East* (GHP, 2006)

Ritson, Darren W., *In Search of Ghosts: Real Hauntings from Around Britain* (GHP, 2007)

Underwood, Peter, *This Haunted Isle* (Harrap, 1984)

Underwood, Peter, *A Gazetteer or British Ghosts* (Souvenir Press, 1971)

Underwood, Peter, *A–Z of British Ghosts* (Souvenir Press, 1971)

A splendid view of the Tyne bridges, taken from the roof of Newcastle Keep.

Other titles published by The History Press

Haunted Northumberland
DARREN W. RITSON

This fascinating book contains a terrifying collection of true-life, spine-chilling tales from across Northumberland. Featuring stories of unexplained phenomena, apparitions and poltergeists, and including the tale of the Hexham Heads, the Pink Lady of Bamburgh Castle and the ghost of Hadrian's Wall, this book is guaranteed to make your blood run cold.

978 0 7524 5861 8

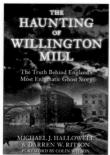

The Haunting of Willington Mill:
The Truth Behind England's Most Enigmatic Ghost Story
MICHAEL J. HALLOWELL & DARREN W. RITSON

During the nineteenth century, Willington Mill gained an infamous reputation. Bizarre noises, apparitions and poltergeist activity dogged the premises and were experienced by dozens of credible witnesses. The case attracted the interest of the country's leading psychical researchers of the time, but the mystery was never solved – until now. Within these pages the true story of Willington Mill, one of England's most enigmatic and puzzling hauntings, is finally pieced together.

978 0 7524 5878 6

Ghosts at Christmas
DARREN W. RITSON

From Charles Dickens' famous *A Christmas Carol* to Tim Burton's *The Nightmare Before Christmas*, the festive season has long been closely associated with ghostly tales. In this fascinating work, Darren W. Ritson looks not only at the fictional treatment of Christmas ghosts but also at a host of true-life stories from across the country. Featuring accounts of unexplained phenomena, apparitions and poltergeists, this book will entertain and terrify in equal measure.

978 0 7524 5767 3

Haunted Berwick
DARREN W. RITSON

This fascinating book contains a terrifying collection of true-life tales from around Berwick. Take a tour of this ancient town and discover an unnerving assortment of poltergeists, spectres and myths, including a witch's curse, the warning toll of a ghostly bell, chilling vampiric encounters, and the inauspicious spirit of a weeping boy. Containing many tales which have never before been published, *Haunted Berwick* will delight and thrill everyone interested in the paranormal.

978 0 7524 5548 8

Visit our website and discover thousands of other History Press books.
www.thehistorypress.co.uk

The
History
Press